Shopping with Clara

a journal of letting go

beth krietzman

Shopping with Clara

ISBN 13: 978-1-59298-873-0

Library of Congress Catalog Number: 2015906071

Printed in the United States of America

First Printing: 2015

19 18 17 16 15   5 4 3 2 1

Cover and interior design by Laura Drew.
Illustration of Beth and Clara by Abbey Road.

Beaver's Pond Press
7108 Ohms Lane
Edina, MN 55439–2129
952-829-8818
www.beaverspondpress.com

BEAVER'S POND
PRESS

For Clara

Preface

I have dyslexia and anxiety.

My brain processes information differently than other people's brains do, and I struggle with the fact that I cannot always understand things that I read or things that people say. I have an extremely difficult time putting concepts in sequence, and cannot organize my thoughts easily. It is challenging for me to express myself both verbally and in writing. I also worry about everything.

Growing up with this disability made things very difficult for me. I struggled to keep up in class, constantly wondering why I just didn't get it. I was always in the slow reading and math groups. I could never understand why I could not do math like the other kids. I had to use my fingers to count, even for the simplest problems. Math word problems were the worst. A problem a regular student could solve in about one minute took me twenty minutes of drawing pictures and making charts. I remember multiplication-tables tests causing me some of the biggest stress. I have vivid memories of the other students turning over their completed tests while I was still on the first couple of lines, having to count on my fingers.

Reading wasn't any better. The task of having to stand up in front of the class made me feel like I was going to be sick. I was embarrassed because I couldn't read as well as the other students. I despised those reading comprehension tests where I had to read the story and then answer the questions. When it came time to answer the questions, it was as if I had never even read the story!

I was three years into college when I finally found out that I had dyslexia. Having an explanation for my difficulties did help—in a way. I was given special services to help with my studying, reading, and tests. I somehow graduated college, and even made it through graduate school.

Being an adult with dyslexia brings another set of challenges for me. To put it simply, I have to work twice as hard at everything I do. Analyzing, organizing, listening, reading, and writing all take extra time. I have to check and recheck everything I do, to make sure I haven't made a mistake. Helping my kids with schoolwork is entertaining for them. I have to go through the process of drawing pictures and making charts to help them with math problems. They're amused by my teaching techniques. Having dyslexia is very frustrating. However, I have learned to cope with it and appreciate the unusual way my brain works.

My dyslexia—with all its history, the tangents it leads me on, the accompanying anxiety, and the way it shapes the way I think and express myself—is a part of this story, but only one part of it. The rest didn't come together until I met Clara. This journal is our story, of two unusual people brought together by chance—although sometimes I wonder if it was chance at all—and the friendship that changed both of our lives.

I once told Clara I was going to write a book about our adventures shopping. She laughed and said, "What's so interesting about our shopping?" *You have no idea!* I thought. And she didn't. Clara was funny, smart, stubborn, and often difficult. Yet I found my time with Clara to be surprisingly fitting for me. I saw myself, at times, in her. Often I was downright frustrated with her, wondering if perhaps she gave me a glimpse into my own future.

Introductions

One of my first experiences with people who take care of the elderly was shortly after my grandfather died, when my grandmother was left alone. My grandma had a few caregivers who would do things for her, such as take her shopping and to appointments, and they provided her with needed companionship. I remember feeling a sense of admiration for them and their dedication to the elderly. I felt that someday I would like to do similar work.

I happen to talk with my neighbor Jan one afternoon when she mentions that she volunteers through the Jewish Family and Children's Service (JFCS) as an outreach visitor for the elderly, and that they are in need of more volunteers. I tell Jan that I am interested in volunteering. She gives me the contact information for the JFCS. The next day, I email the JFCS and make an appointment with Beverly, the volunteer coordinator.

During my meeting with her, Beverly asks me what kind of a client I would like to work with and what I would enjoy doing as a volunteer. I tell her, "I like grocery shopping. I enjoy walking. And I don't mind running errands, since I am always doing that anyway." I can't help but hope that I will be able to do something that will keep me active. I always feel as if I should be moving and keeping busy.

"I am interested in someone who enjoys running errands and doing things," Beverly says, and she tells me that she will let me know when I am approved as a volunteer and when she finds a client who might be a match.

With personal references from my good friends Meryl and Jan, and a clear background check, I am accepted as an outreach volunteer. Within a few weeks I receive a call from Beverly. She tells me about an elderly woman who has been diagnosed with cancer and lives alone in a retirement community home. She is looking for some companionship. I tell Beverly, "Sure."

The next day, Beverly emails me with another option.

"There is another elderly woman. Her name is Clara and she is also looking for companionship."

I ask Beverly "Which of the two women has family?" It is important to me that I help someone who does not have a lot of support. I want to do something special for someone who doesn't have much.

Beverly tells me that Clara has no immediate relatives, other than a distant cousin. I feel sad for her, being elderly and not having a close family.

I choose Clara.

I next receive an email with her bio:

Clara, 92.

Has trouble hearing.

Emergency contact: Joy.

Clara is looking for help shopping. Friends have passed away.

"Hmm, shopping . . . this is going to work," I say aloud as I read about this woman.

By the end of the week, I receive a phone call from Allison, the social worker from the JFCS who is assigned to Clara. We pick a date and a time to meet at Clara's apartment. I feel both excited and nervous. I tell my family I'm going to meet Clara. Ted, my husband, is outwardly enthusiastic about my new adventure. However, I know what he's thinking. He always tells me that I do too much, and wonders why I continually add to my plate. Margie, my oldest daughter, senses my nervousness and offers to come with me.

When I tell my two younger daughters about my plans to help Clara, they both look at me like I'm crazy. They, like Ted, wonder why I'm adding more volunteer work to my already-busy schedule. After brushing off my family's comments, I start planning for my first meeting with Clara. So many things cross my mind. First, what should I wear? Should I dress fancy? *My clothes can't be too dark—that's depressing—or too light, since that makes me look washed out. Should I wear my hair straight or curly?* It's funny what we try to do in life to show off and make a wonderful first impression, only to laugh later at our vain silliness.

I am a complete wreck about what clothes to wear. Better yet, I can't decide if I should I wear deodorant and makeup. *Should I or shouldn't I?* It sounds like a silly question with an obvious answer, but along with my dyslexia and anxiety, I also have strange allergies. My body is allergic to deodorant, makeup, sugar, salt, dust, and certain chemicals. If I wear deodorant, my armpits will itch for weeks. If I wear makeup, my eyes will burn and tear through the entire meeting. How can I *not* wear makeup, though? I'll look unprofessional at worst, and blah at best.

During my freshman year of college, the boys in my dorm would often tease me, saying I looked like their grandmas when I didn't wear makeup. I took the teasing more seriously than I probably should have; the first year of college is one of those times in an impressionable girl's life that shapes who she becomes as an adult. When getting ready to go out, I'd often ask myself, "Should I allow my body to itch and burn? Or should I look like grandma?" At eighteen, I was terrified of looking that old, so I was almost always uncomfortable. At forty-eight, I'm still not yet ready to look that old.

For the meeting with Clara, I settle on itchy armpits and runny eyes.

My meeting with Clara is set for January 6, 2011 at 11:00 a.m. When Allison gives me these details, she tells me it's difficult to get into the building.

Thursday, January 6, 2011

I arrive at 10:45 a.m. because I'm always early. As a child, I learned never to be late for anything, or else I would suffer *"the wrath of Mom."* Adhering to my mom's orders about being on time set the foundation for who I am now. The way I was raised taught me some important lessons. I think being on time, or early, is one of those lessons.

I meet Allison in the lobby. I quickly realize that she is the quiet type of person. She is dressed professionally in a black pantsuit. Her hair is long, straight, and brown, and she is a few inches taller than I am. She is very pretty.

Allison seems a bit lost at the building. *Has she been here before?* Despite Allison's concerns about getting into the building, we have no trouble. From the phone in the lobby, Allison calls the number to Clara's apartment, and I make a mental note of how to do this, knowing I will likely be alone the next time I visit Clara. I have to admit that I'm nervous. I'm sweating and I smell—*as usual*. I'm wearing deodorant and it's not even working. Hopefully

Clara's senses are dulled at ninety-two and she won't notice.

As we go up the elevator to the second floor, Allison and I talk about the day. I'm trying to make more mental notes about how to get to the apartment for next time. I worry about everything, although not finding her apartment is a silly worry—but I worry, regardless. Allison knocks on the door. We wait a long time for Clara to answer. She finally does, and there stands this woman. I'm a little shocked. She's old. Really old! My first thought is of Beetlejuice, the character from Tim Burton's 1988 movie.

Clara has thick-rimmed glasses, which make her eyeballs appear much larger than their actual size. Her hair is white, stiff, and in a traditional bowl cut. Her clothes are the typical polyester pants and top that would have been worn in the 1960s. She has white socks and those slip-on shoes that old people wear, shoes that look like you could fall over while wearing them. Her teeth are large, yellow, and crooked. She has white hairs on her chin. After standing there for a moment, Clara finally tells us, in a firm but polite way, to come in and sit down. I sense immediately that I'm not dealing with a regular old-grandma type.

Her apartment has an interesting smell, kind of like a forgotten meal left on the stove and paper bags that have been left rotting in a puddle of water. I can see thick layers of dust along the counters and baseboards. With my allergies, I'm sensitive to this. I perpetually clean my own home to make sure it doesn't gather dust and to ease my anxiety of having a dirty home. As I look around, I feel queasy, wondering how long it's been since her apartment has been cleaned, *if it has ever been cleaned.* The couch is old, blue, and saggy. All the pictures on the walls are crooked. Papers are piled everywhere on the dining room table. I'm not sure I can do this. My worry isn't even about my first impression of Clara, but rather that, with all my anxieties, I don't know if I can physically survive coming over here with any frequency.

Allison introduces the both of us, and I can tell Clara is trying to size me up, as I am doing with her. With Clara's diminished hearing and lack of a hearing aid, she can't hear what Allison and I are saying. We have to almost shout for her to hear us, and Allison doesn't seem to be a good shouter. She is so soft-spoken that I don't think Clara can hear what she's saying. I'm doing a better job at shouting than Allison is, but of course, I have teenagers, and talking loudly tends to come naturally to any parent with teenagers. I wonder if Allison has any kids.

Apparently, Clara won't use a hearing aid due to the cost and the fact that they never seemed to work when she wore them before.

"So, what would you like to do?" I ask. We're in an awkward situation and I'm not sure what to say or do. I'm still trying to recover from my first impression, and I don't think I'm doing a good job.

"Maybe a little shopping," Clara replies in a polite, yet not really nice voice. "I need a new purse and maybe a new nightgown." *Why at ninety-two does she want a new purse?* It's a fleeting thought, quickly lost when Clara looks over at me and says that I am small, and that she was expecting someone older.

Great; she already doesn't like me. Allison explains to Clara that the JFCS is short on outreach visitors and that they're lucky to have me as a volunteer. I feel awkward being judged like that, knowing that I have no background doing this type of work, but then again, what have I been doing with Clara since I walked in the door? I've been judging her. The thought that I'm doing the same to her as she is to me calms me a little and helps me feel more at ease. After a short visit, Clara and I set our first date for next Wednesday, January 12. I suggest nine o'clock in the morning.

"That's too early. Why are you up so early, anyway?" Clara asks in a firm and almost accusing voice, as if I'm doing something wrong.

"I have kids in school and need to be home by one o'clock in the afternoon," I tell her.

We agree on Wednesday at ten thirty. *Why Wednesday?* I find out later that it's double coupon day at some of the local grocery stores.

I don't know it at this point, but my book is about to be written. Had I known what I was about to get myself into, I'm not sure I would have signed on.

Wednesday, January 12, 2011

Today is our first day together, and I'm driving my family's black station wagon. My choices of transportation are our truck, which I know Clara won't be able to get into due to its height off the ground; our sedan, which my older daughter drives; and lastly, the station wagon. The wagon is definitely the most sensible.

I think it would be appropriate to call Clara before I leave my house. She answers with a drawn out, "Hallow . . ." as if my call is completely unexpected.

"Hi, Clara. It's Beth, your volunteer."

"Who?" she says into the phone.

I repeat louder and more slowly, "BETH, YOUR VOLUNTEER!"

We go back and forth like this until she finally realizes who I am. "Are you here?" she eventually asks.

"No, but I will be there in fifteen minutes."

She says, "I'll go downstairs."

When I arrive, I see through the building's front window that Clara is in the lobby, waiting for me.

I'm not sure what I should do. I suddenly realize how much I *don't* know about this kind of work. What am I allowed to do? What am I not allowed to do? I get out of my car, walk up the steep steps to Clara's building, and help her down the same steps and into my car. Clara holds on to the door as I try to help her keep her balance while she gets in. As I'm trying to close the passenger door, she motions for the seat belt. I realize she isn't able to reach and grab it in order to pull it around her body, so I pull the buckle out and hand it to her. I close the door, walk to the driver's side, and get in. I note that she is a big woman—not overweight, but thicker, tall, broad-shouldered, and stronger than many elderly women. I picture her in her younger years as a stocky farm girl.

I realize, from the way she walked out to the car, there aren't going to be any long walks—ever.

Once we are situated, Clara mentions that she likes the car and asks who drives it. I tell her that my husband usually drives this car.

"I had to switch cars with him because I wasn't sure you would be able to get up and down in my truck, since it's so high off the ground."

"Are you a good driver?" she asks, and I'm caught completely off guard. I can't help but feel like she is still judging me. *I have to be on my best driving behavior.*

I look at Clara. "Where to?" I ask, trying to sound casual and in control.

In a nice, polite voice, she responds, "Well, I would like to go to Cub Foods today." *Five minutes down the road. Easy enough, I think.* Off to Cub we go.

"Can you bring me to the front and drop me off?" Clara asks. It's an innocent enough request, so I pull up to the front door of the grocery store. "Can you get closer to the door?" she then asks.

If I get any closer, we'll be in the door. I hate blocking the entrance so other people can't get in. I stop the car close to the door and help her out. After I park the car, I go into the store as quickly as I can. I'm not sure what to expect.

She is sitting in one of those grocery store scooters that has a basket attached to the front. Clara is repeatedly pressing the "go" button, but nothing happens, so I flag down an employee who tells us we need to unplug the scooter before it will work. I unplug the scooter and off she goes, with me trying to keep up behind her.

She asks me if I plan to do some shopping, too. I'm not sure *what* I'm going to do. I had been so focused on just getting Clara going that I hadn't thought about what I'd do while Clara shopped. I assumed I would walk around with her. However, that seems a bit awkward, just following her around. I grab my own cart and head to the fruit and vegetables with her.

So many thoughts cross my mind. *How does this whole thing work? Do I help her? Or does she do this on her own?* Clara starts asking people for help getting bags and food. I quickly realize that she doesn't just want company while shopping; she actually needs help with her shopping. I tear off a bunch of bags from the dispenser and slide them through one of the holes in the basket on her cart so they are within her reach.

Clara drives that scooter so dang fast that I can hardly keep up. She whizzes around corners and knocks over displays, and I chase alongside, cleaning up after her. A woman stops me to ask if I take Clara shopping often. I kindly tell her that it is my first day. The woman says I am doing a wonderful thing, and I thank her. Since it is my first day with Clara and I'm very nervous, the acknowledgment from the woman helps to calm me.

From the fruits and vegetables, I follow Clara to the fish. She is touching all the fish packages, lifting and scrutinizing each plastic-wrapped piece. She puts them down and then she starts all over again with all the fish that she has already examined. She turns the packages sideways and looks at them from every angle. *Oh no; this is not going to work for me!* I'm a germ freak. I begin to panic, knowing that I am going to have to touch those packages. More importantly, her hands are now contaminated with bacteria. How can I ask her to clean them?

I run to the nearest bag dispenser and tear off another handful of bags. I run back and use the bags to handle the fish package she selects. I'm not going to touch the package with *my* bare hands. As I place the bagged fish into her basket, she gives me a funny look. There's no way I'm telling her that I'm afraid of germs.

I trace this fear back to my first experience with food poisoning, which I vividly remember. I was twelve and with my family on a ski vacation in Michigan. At exactly 2:00 a.m. one morning, my sister and I woke with horrible stomach pains, and we raced frantically to the bathroom. We stood there, staring at each other, wondering how we were both going to use the same toilet at the same time. We were terribly sick for many hours—my sister with diarrhea and me with vomiting. In fact, our parents felt that we were sick enough to be taken to a hospital in town near the ski resort.

I remember lying on what looked like a creepy, old operating table, and the nurse coming at me with a needle longer then my arm, injecting Compazine (I have never forgotten that name) right into my butt cheek. The pain radiated through my entire body. My sister was lucky enough to just get a pill to stop her diarrhea. I was scared of taking pills, though, because I had a difficult time swallowing them, so I was stuck with the shot.

After we left the hospital, I had to endure a nauseating eight-hour drive home to Minnesota, flopping around like a rubber chicken in my brother's army-style Jeep. My sister got the better ride in my parents' station wagon. The soreness from that horrible shot lasted three months, and I was convinced my butt was permanently damaged. Ever since then, I have been petrified of food poisoning and of getting sick. I know that Clara won't understand, so I tell her that I don't want the fish package to leak in the paper grocery bag. She accepts my explanation.

As we move on to the kosher meat section, things only get worse for me. Clara continues to do the same analysis of the red meat and chicken that she has done with the fish. Only now she is setting all the packages in her lap after each analysis. *This cannot be happening!* She has a large stack of meat packages in her lap and on her clothes. I'm anxious and grossed out. How can I let her back into my car? Clara will think I'm nuts if I make her drive the scooter to the bathroom and clean her hands. Maybe I should get some wipes and clean her hands. I decide not to bother; she'd never understand.

My panic with Clara isn't extraordinary. Every day I struggle with my anxieties about raw meats and vegetables. I cook chicken until it's rubber because I'm afraid someone will get salmonella. I wash my hands several times a day. I can't bear to touch door handles and I carry special gloves in my car that I use at gas stations and banks. I call them my gas gloves. My time with Clara will clearly be a challenge.

Clara's next items are jumbo eggs and a gallon of Kemps Select milk. She pulls out a grocery list and a blue pocketbook with coupons that she's categorized alphabetically. I wonder why she hadn't taken out her shopping list earlier. We have to make our way back to the fruits and vegetables to get the items on her list that she didn't get when we were there the first time. After another round of fruits and vegetables, we head toward the cereal aisle. On our way, Clara knocks over several displays, ignoring the fallen items as if nothing happened. I scramble to pick up the boxes while racing after Clara, trying to keep up. I am somewhere between laughing at myself and blushing in embarrassment.

Clara selects Total cereal. It is on sale, five boxes for $9.00. I also notice she has a coupon for the cereal. I guess she's going to stock up because it's on sale. She next wants toilet paper. The paper can't be double rolls, but only single rolls, she tells me. "Why?" I ask. She says that she can't fit the double rolls on the bar in her bathroom. When we find what she wants, she says, "Toilet paper is too expensive today. I'll let it go." I think to myself, *If you need toilet paper, you better get it*, but I don't say anything. Our next stop is for canned vegetables. The cans are on sale, and she has a coupon.

After we finish shopping and return back to her building, I carry the groceries up to her apartment. I take them out of the bags, and Clara tells me to leave them on the counter. She says she will put them away. Her kitchen is the size and shape that you would expect in a small apartment; it's rectangular, cramped, and a bit depressing. It's in the 1970s style, with the dated, dark, oak cabinetry; the entire space is cluttered with plastic and paper bags. My shoes stick to the laminate floor. Yuck; I can only imagine what's causing it. Looking around, I see no sign of soap or towels to wash my hands with. I don't know what to do, so I don't do anything.

We set a date for Wednesday of the following week, and I leave. I sanitize my hands as soon as I get in the car.

Interesting first visit, I think to myself as I sit in my car, disinfecting from germs. Clara enjoys grocery shopping; she's just like the kind of person I requested as a match. This situation may be okay after all—*other than the germ problem*. I wonder what it'll be like the next time. I go home and spray the car with Lysol disinfectant.

Clara has touched everything in my car. It is definitely contaminated. I have to clean.

Wednesday, January 19, 2011

I call Clara before I leave my house. It's the same thing as last week.

She answers with a drawn out "Hallow . . ."

"Hi, Clara. It's Beth, your volunteer."

"Who?" she shouts into the phone.

I repeat louder and more slowly, "BETH, YOUR VOLUNTEER!"

We go back and forth like this until she finally realizes who I am. "Are you here?" she asks. I respond no, and tell her that I will be there in fifteen minutes. She says, "I'll go downstairs."

When I arrive, Clara is waiting for me in her lobby. I get out of my car and help her down the steep steps. I don't know why they had to build steps this steep. It's hard for someone like Clara to go up and down them. I get her in the car and pull the buckle around her. She tells me that she wants to go to Cub Foods again today.

In the car, Clara tells me a little about her childhood. She grew up on the Iron Range in northern Minnesota.

Her mom loved to cook large meals. Clara would walk a half-mile home from school each day for lunch. Her mom would make a huge meal of meat and potatoes. I'm guessing she looked not unlike I pictured; in fact, she comments that she was fat as a child.

Her father owned a grocery store where she spent many days. I am getting to know a little about Clara, even if it is only small quips and comments. It is only a little information, but the feeling I have about her sharing puts a smile on my face. It's hard to imagine this ninety-two-year-old woman as a young girl, but I guess, when we look at our own grandparents, we don't think that at one time they were our own age. As young people they had dreams, lives, and secrets we likely will never know about. It is fun to hear about Clara—a young girl, a small town, and a grocery store.

When we get to Cub Foods, I drop her at the door and go park the car. Upon entering the store, I find her in the scooter, trying to get it to start. I remind her that we have to unplug it before it will work. I unplug it, and once again she's off. In my opinion, she drives the scooter way too fast. If they gave out speeding tickets at the grocery store, Clara would get one. I wonder if she was a fast driver when she drove a car.

I tear off a handful of bags and chase her down. Like last week, I put some bags through the hole in the basket on her scooter. Her selection of food is very similar to last week. Clara picks about five or six roma tomatoes over the other varieties because they are the cheapest. She then gets romaine lettuce, a bag of potatoes, and a bag of onions.

We next stop at the fish. I'm ready with more bags! She does the same analysis, inspecting the packages from every angle. She sees that the fish was imported from Chile and that color was added. She shakes her head and drives away. Next stop is the meats. She does the same inspection of the packages. It feels like we are at the kosher meats forever. However, she does not select any meat today. We move on to juice, cottage cheese, milk, and eggs. She finally takes out her coupons, and she has several. We stop in each aisle and get all the items that she has coupons for.

After we finish shopping, I drive her back to her apartment and help her out of the car. I take the groceries out of the car and put them in the lobby. Clara gets her mail from the box in the lobby and waits for me to park the car. We take the elevator to her apartment. She takes off her boots and jacket and immediately walks to a blue-and-white-striped chair in her living room. She sits, then turns on the TV while I unpack the groceries. When I finish, I sit on the couch and we talk about my kids. She wants to know their names and how old they are. I stay for about thirty minutes and then leave.

Wednesday, January 26, 2011

I call Clara to tell her that I am on my way. She tells me her lamp isn't working and we need to take it to a hardware store. I tell her I will look at it when I get there.

I call Clara from the lobby and she buzzes me in from her phone. I don't know why, but I'm surprised she's able to buzz me in on the first call. Before we leave to go shopping, I ask Clara where the lamp is that isn't working. I want to check it just in case we have to take it somewhere for repair. She shows me the lamp in her bedroom, and I try to turn it on. It doesn't work. I take the lamp to the living room and plug it in, and it works. I tell her the problem might be the outlet in the bedroom. I have another look and find the light switch in her bedroom has been turned off and there is no power in the room. I explain she has probably turned the power switch off, which would affect the outlet. Clara disagrees with me. She doesn't think she turned the light switch off.

"Maybe it was the cleaning woman," she says.

I think that it was probably Clara who turned off the switch.

Grocery shopping today is very similar to our last outing. Her selection of foods is always the same, it seems; at least it's healthy. I'm glad to see that she eats well and cooks fresh foods for herself. However, I do wonder if she likes eating the same things each week or if she just selects these same items because of their prices. She is a bit obsessed with tomatoes, eating two to three pounds each week. Clara has me thinking about tomatoes. I wonder if I should be eating more.

After shopping and before I leave her place, we sit down and look at the calendar. Clara tells me she has a pacemaker checkup and blood test appointments next week. I need to take her to both. She wants me to pick her up at 9:30 a.m. because her appointment is at 9:45. I tell her I will be at her apartment at 9:30.

I am busy in my life outside of Clara. My life is like a circus, with different rings of things going on at the same time. Sometimes I feel like a juggling clown. I am a part-time accountant, I teach kindergarten Sunday school, and I substitute as a preschool teacher. My three children are each involved in three different activities, sports, and/or clubs. I sit on the booster clubs of several of their sports teams.

I also volunteer at the high school in the ceramics class. I don't do ceramics, though, and I think it's funny that I help in the class when I have never thrown a pot or made any type of ceramic. But I couldn't pass up the opportunity to help.

When I was at the open house at the high school in the fall, I met the ceramics teacher. She mentioned that she needed help and was always on the lookout for volunteers. I had volunteered at both the elementary school and junior high, so I thought it would be great to help at the high school as well. Margie loves tracking me down when I'm in the class. She takes ceramics, and the classroom is her home away from home.

On top of all the work I do, I also have a large dog that needs to be walked every day and a cat that constantly follows me around the house meowing for food. Ted calls my job "home management." Adding Clara into the mix—now that I realize what she needs me to do for her—I wonder if I really have the time to volunteer. Despite that thought, I can't quit now; I've just started.

I made a commitment to volunteering with Clara, and I cannot let her down. When I consider leaving her, I worry about "what if"s. What if I quit now? What will happen to Clara? What will she do? What if she can't find someone else to take her shopping? I can think of a hundred "what if"s. I can't stop thinking of them.

And anyway, I can't seem to let things go once I start them. I feel responsible and somehow feel a sense of ownership; when I start something, it becomes my own, in a way. I think that not giving up on things has to do with my dyslexia and having to work so hard to overcome obstacles when I was young. I've done that for so long that it's now a part of my personality.

Like everything else that I do, I will somehow make the adjustment and fit Clara in. Clara and I are just getting to know each other and getting used to our weekly shopping routine. Besides, I would feel sad for Clara if she had to go through the process of adjusting to a new volunteer all over again—and so soon. I have a sense that it would bother her.

Wednesday, February 2, 2011

Clara makes an odd noise, one that I began to notice
during our second visit. It sounds almost like there is a
motor buzzing or humming in her body. I stare at her
when I hear the noise to see if I can figure out where it's
coming from. Since I first noticed it, I have wondered
if the noise has something to do with her pacemaker.
I'm the kind of person who has to have an answer for
everything, so the fact that I cannot figure out the source
of the noise is bothering me. I recently asked my friend
Jan, who is a doctor, about it. She told me that you
cannot hear a motor sound from a pacemaker. At some
point I may have to ask Clara herself where the noise is
coming from, just to satisfy my own curiosity.

I pick Clara up at nine thirty for the pacemaker
checkup appointment. On the way to the appointment,
Clara tells me that the pacemaker they put in her was
a "closeout" model, and that the doctors gave her that
particular model because she is old. Clara feels they don't
want to waste the good ones on someone who is likely to
die sooner rather than later. *Such a morbid thought*, I think,
but don't say out loud.

I drop her off at the door at the hospital. I make sure she has my cell phone number and knows to have a nurse call me when she is finished. They have a valet service with a wheelchair to bring her inside the clinic. I will pick her up at the same door. I decide to make use of my free time and run to the grocery store for a few things. I find it's easier not to do my own grocery shopping as I help Clara with hers. It's too difficult for me to help her and look for my own things.

The nurse calls me while I'm on my way back to the hospital. Clara is done and ready for me to pick her up. When I arrive, Clara gets in the car and we drive to her blood-work appointment. I drop her off at the door, since the building has valet service similar to the hospital's. It takes me forever to park because the ramp is so full. I have to drive all the way to the top to get a spot. I run down the stairs to get to the clinic, and find Clara in a crowded waiting area. I try to talk to Clara, but she cannot hear me, so I have to shout. The people around us turn and listen.

We wait about thirty to forty minutes before they call her name. It takes less than five minutes for them to draw her blood, and we leave soon after she is called. Our next stop is Cub Foods.

As I'm helping Clara, a woman stops me and asks what my relationship to Clara is. The woman is very curious about my volunteer time with Clara and questions me on how I got involved. She tells me that she has an elderly mother who needs help with things like shopping. The woman wants to know where to get information about getting a volunteer. I bet there are many people who are interested in getting help for their elderly family members and don't know where to start. As the woman walks away, she tells me that I'm doing a good thing. It's nice to hear. I smile, knowing that I really am helping someone— Clara.

I bring Clara and her groceries back to her apartment and unpack the groceries, as I usually do. Before I leave, Clara asks if I would like to go to lunch next week. *Hmm, this is interesting.* I wonder why she wants to have lunch. Is she interested in a friendship, or is it her way of showing gratitude for my volunteering? Is she going to want to pay for my lunch? I'm uncomfortable with this. She does not have much, and I don't want her spending money on me. We decide that next week we will first shop and then have lunch.

She tells me that she wants to go to Byerly's, a grocery store that has a restaurant, so she can have the salad bar. I don't like eating at restaurants, and salad bars make me a bit nervous. Again, I'm afraid of getting sick. It grosses me out when people touch everything, like when they use the utensils and then put them back. The handles usually touch the food. I've seen individuals at grocery stores reach their hands into a dish after the spoon is completely immersed in order to pull the spoon out. With my worries about Clara paying and my obsession with germs and cleanliness, the thought of going out to lunch makes me nervous. However, I will go for Clara.

Wednesday, February 9, 2011

I pick up Clara and we go to Cub Foods to shop. As planned, we then go to Byerly's for lunch. At Byerly's we sit down at our table and Clara orders the salad bar. I order a bowl of oatmeal. Clara gives me a look of disgust and, in an irritated voice, tells me that I have not ordered enough food. She is clearly appalled by my eating habits. Given her tone of voice, it's almost as if I have offended her.

I tell her, "I don't eat much for lunch because I get too tired after I eat." I'm still not comfortable with Clara knowing about my anxieties.

Clara proceeds to the salad bar with a curmudgeonly look on her face, and I follow to help her. Before now, I have never seen Clara eat. I gather she is a big eater because of her groceries, and by what she has told me about her eating habits as a child. However, I am still shocked when I see her pile every possible fruit and vegetable that she can onto her plate.

I order toast with my oatmeal to make it look like I eat more, although I know that won't suffice. Just looking at Clara's plate, I know that, unless I fill my own plate, I won't be able to get Clara's approval. She seems to scrutinize everything I do—not necessarily by saying something, but with a certain look in her eyes—like when she examines the groceries in my cart at the store. I'm bothered by the fact that I worry about whether or not she approves of what I buy or eat. I don't know why I feel this way; I just do. Throughout our entire lunch, she seems to keep getting mad at me, telling me I should eat more. She stares at me, as if I am doing something wrong.

Clara's scrutiny brings back memories of my childhood and my mom's rules about food. Our family meals were anything but relaxing. My mom was a terrible cook, and my siblings and I could barely stomach the food she made. She would make what she called "hamburgers on the grill." They were more like burnt baseballs. I could never understand why she could not flatten them so they would fit in buns. Even if they did fit in the buns, we could not eat them because of how hard they were. She also often made a revolting family steak that required us to chew like it was a rubber dog toy; it smelled like a person's flesh. And then there were the canned waxed or string beans that were our daily accompanying vegetable. Noncooking days were filled in with Kentucky Fried Chicken, McDonald's, Burger King, TV dinners, or cereal.

When it came to eating, my mom was both the "chief of time" and the "police of food." She would dictate who could eat what and when. We were never allowed to open the refrigerator or have a snack of any kind unless it was at my mom's set times. Breakfast—8:00 a.m. Snack—10:00 a.m. Lunch—11:30 a.m. Snack—2:00 p.m. Dinner—5:00 p.m. Snack—7:00 p.m. There was absolutely no bending of these rules. I swear my mom had supersonic ears, because even from outside the house she could hear the sound of the refrigerator opening.

Clara seems to work for the "police of food," too. She eats every bit of food on her plate.

After our attempt at eating lunch together, we go back to her apartment, where Clara tells me that her television remote doesn't work very well. She sits down in her blue-and-white-striped chair while I check the remote. I suggest that I could buy batteries, put the new ones in, and see how it goes.

Wednesday, February 16, 2011

I put new batteries in Clara's TV remote, and it seems to work fine. She's happy. Clara tells me her boots are torn. They're the old type of black galoshes that have side zippers. My guess is they're from the 1970s, maybe even earlier. She tells me that her feet are big and she needs a men's size ten. She says she's called around, but doesn't think anyone still carries the same kind.

Being the avid researcher I am, I do my own investigation. I call around, looking for the boots. After a few tries, I accept the fact that Clara is right; no one seems to carry the boots, or anything similar. Per Clara's request, we pay a visit to a shoe store not far from her apartment. She tries on several available options and none seem to fit well enough.

In the short time we've spent together, I've gotten to know Clara's tendencies pretty well. Regardless of whether or not she tries boots on, I know she will never spend the money on new boots. I offer to use black duct tape and tape hers up. If she isn't going to buy new boots, then something has to be done to fix her old ones. It's winter, and winter in Minnesota can be cold and snowy. She says she'll think about it. I later go out and buy the duct tape, knowing she will eventually have me tape them.

Wednesday, February 23, 2011

When I pick up Clara, she tells me she wants a haircut.
"Okay, where should we go?" I ask. "Well, I have a
coupon for a hair salon," she says. I'm curious about the
style she's going to choose for her hair. Her hair is always
kind of messy—scarecrowlike, you might say. So I'm not
quite sure what the style is. I take her to the salon, which
is not more than five minutes from her apartment. It's one
of those inexpensive chain-store salons you can find at
any mall in the country. I sit and wait while she gets her
haircut.

The young gentleman cutting her hair is having a
hard time communicating with Clara, so I go over to the
chair and try to help. The stylist has a thick accent and is
soft-spoken. He wants to know what kind of style Clara
wants. I tell him she can't hear well and that he has to talk
louder. I end up translating back and forth between the
two of them. The end result is a very short bowl cut. It
literally looks like he put a bowl on her head and trimmed
around the edges. No wash, no water. Just a plain old
dry cut. Clara looks in the mirror and gives her nod of

approval. She must be okay with the results, because she doesn't make any negative comment. I have begun to learn that Clara speaks up when she's not happy with something. Clara's hair looks much better.

Coupon time. What a deal: a haircut for $8.00.

After her haircut, we go grocery shopping at Cub Foods. I then bring her back to her apartment and unpack her groceries. While I'm busy in the kitchen, Clara sits in her chair and calls me into the living room. As I expected, she asks if I will tape her boots. It just so happens that I have the duct tape with me—prepared, I am.

I know I will have to tape carefully. I have noticed that Clara can be quite fussy, and I sense that she has an edge to her; it's as if she will snap or explode at any time. Maybe it's the look on her face, or the shake of her head when she does not approve of the selections at the grocery store, or her huffy mannerisms when I help her in and out of my car; I'm not sure. But I don't want to upset her. I tape carefully, inside and out, taking my time to perfectly slide the tape along the zigzag tear. When I'm done, the lines don't match exactly, but Clara doesn't seem to mind. She is happy to have her boots back together again.

Before I leave, Clara shows me that the remote to her television is not working again. I notice that when she pushes the button, it takes a few times for the remote and television to align. The problem must be with the remote and not the batteries I had replaced a couple weeks ago. She may need a new remote. I tell Clara that I will check some stores to see if I can find her a new one.

Knowing how frugal Clara is, I call around to find out who has the best deal on TV remotes. However, I'm not even certain she will approve of my buying the cheapest one. Her television is likely the most prized item she has; she spends much of her day watching it. After several calls, I eventually find a remote with large buttons. I hope I don't make a mistake in getting the cheapest I can find. It's only $12.00, but if the remote doesn't work, it will almost be as bad to Clara as if I had purchased the most expensive remote I could find. The instructions say it will work for all TVs. I cross my fingers as I pay for it and walk out of the store, my heart racing, hoping it will work, and knowing how she will react if it doesn't.

Wednesday, March 2, 2011

After I unload Clara's groceries from our usual shopping trip, I start to get nervous. I'm anxious, knowing I'll have to program her television for her with the new remote that I purchased. With Clara, I never know exactly how she'll react. I don't want to get her mad. I always try to pretend I'm confident and know what I'm doing when I'm with her, but I wonder if she can see through me to the truth. The truth is, I'm not always confident in what I do.

This goes back to my school days, when I never felt smart enough, no matter what I did. I tried to hide what I did not know at the time was a disability. I really wanted to learn and understand things as well as the other students did. In first grade, for example, I wanted the gold and silver stars on my spelling tests like all the other students received. They were the stars that came on a sheet, that the teacher had to lick and stick to your paper. Gold was for a perfect score, and silver was for the next best.

Each week after grading our spelling tests, Mrs. S. would lay the tests out on the table for everyone to see.

My test always stood out; it was the one with the red number and a minus next to it. The same kids each week got red numbers, while the rest, which was the majority, got the beautiful gold or silver stars, neatly licked and stuck to their papers.

It wasn't that I didn't study. I studied plenty—probably more than most. I would spend several days during the week sitting with my mom, going over the words. I simply had a difficult time learning them. But I knew them well enough the night before the test. However, the next day, when Mrs. S. would read a word from the list, it was as if someone had erased what was in my brain. The words that I had memorized the night before were suddenly foreign to me. I felt sad and embarrassed bringing my test home each week. I had no explanation for why I got most, if not all, of the words wrong.

When I was in elementary school, no one talked about learning disabilities or dyslexia. Kids who struggled were just considered stupid and placed in the slow reading and math groups. I was a good kid and always wanted to please the teacher. In fact, as a child, I wanted everybody to be happy all the time. To do this, I felt that I had to be perfect and not upset anyone. I felt that I had to hide my dyslexia.

To please Mrs. S., I tried to pretend that I was smart. I loved Mrs. S. I wanted her to see that I was just as smart as the other students. I also wanted a gold star on my paper. I don't remember planning it, but I do remember what I did and what happened. We were taking a spelling test.

Each time Mrs. S. read the word out loud, I carefully—and I thought sneakily—lifted up my desktop and looked at a sheet of paper inside my desk that had the spelling words on it. I was copying the words off my list.

It did not take long for Mrs. S. to catch on. She calmly came over to my desk and asked what I was doing. I don't remember my answer, but it must not have been the right one, because before I could finish my sentence, Mrs. S. flipped my desk over, the contents of which, including the evidence, my cheat sheet, spilled all over the classroom floor. I remember both the mortified looks on the students' faces and their snickering. To say the least, I never cheated again. I was too afraid of being caught. I still am.

I can sense that Clara likes people who are educated. She speaks about her relatives who were lawyers, doctors, and businesspeople. Others she seems to dismiss. Sometimes I feel like I'm not smart enough to be Clara's volunteer. She is like a human calculator who can do math like I've never seen before. I hope she never asks me to do any adding or subtracting for her. I would need a calculator, paper, and pen—or the use of my fingers! I'm always afraid of making a mistake. Maybe I should start carrying a calculator with me, just in case.

Clara calls me the "fix-it person" because I seem to be able to fix everything around her apartment. *I wish I had time to do this at my own house.* I grab the new remote and sit on her living room floor in front of the television. I begin removing it from the package, which is a process in

41

itself. I hate these hard plastic containers. I can't help but feel like I'm going to slice a finger open.

I finally get it open, though, all fingers intact! In the short amount of time I have spent with Clara, I have learned that she is very particular and can be quite opinionated. What if I can't program the remote? What will she say? As I sit on the floor with my legs crossed like a child, staring at the television, I can't help but again wonder what she thinks of me. I'm sure it appears as if I am just playing with the remote, and I am! I'm scared thinking about what I'm going to do if I can't set it up correctly.

Clara sits in her usual blue-and-white-striped chair, staring at me like a schoolteacher ready to correct my work. I read the instructions and begin programming. With my luck—*of course*—it doesn't work. My anxiety starts to mount. *Why do I get so anxious with all of Clara's things?* I take a deep breath to gather my thoughts and continue to fumble between the remote and the instructions. After several tries, I finally get the thing to work. I am so relieved. It works perfectly fine.

It's a simple remote with only a few buttons, all of them large and easy to see and touch. Clara picks up the remote and pushes the buttons, as if she is trying to find something wrong with it. She is checking to make sure her favorite channels get a clear picture. I guess her nod of approval at each channel means my work will suffice.

Wednesday, March 9, 2011

We have the same shopping routine each week. Clara waits for me in the lobby; I get her into the car, and drive to whichever grocery store she requests. I drop her off at the front door and park my car. I then go into the store and find her trying to get the scooter to turn on. I unplug the scooter, and then place a handful of plastic bags through the basket of the scooter for Clara to grab and place her fruits and vegetables in.

Clara makes her usual selections today: several roma tomatoes, potatoes, onions, romaine lettuce, and carrots. As she shops, I catch up with her and see a nice man trying to help her with the scooter. I can see the man is frustrated because he can't get the scooter to work. I know what to do because I've been helping her with the scooter for a couple months now. I get the scooter to work right away, and the man seems a bit embarrassed that he is unable to help. I try to make him feel better by letting him know I've been dealing with the scooter for a long time, and know exactly what the problem is and how to fix it. I don't know if my comment makes him feel any better.

After we shop and return back to her apartment, Clara invites me to sit with her in her den and look at her photo album. I'm excited. I love old family photos, and hearing the history and stories behind them. The album is old and has mostly black-and-white photos. At one point, Clara pauses and points to a baby photo and says it is Bob Dylan. She tells me he is a cousin. I ask her how she is related, exactly. She tells me, but soon after I can't remember. We also run across a photo of Clara with a woman I recognize as my daughters' preschool teacher, Patti. Clara tells me that she volunteered for many years at the preschool. It is strange seeing Clara in the photo with Patti. I wonder if Clara was volunteering at the preschool when my kids were there.

Later, I ask my daughters if they remember a woman like Clara at their school. They say they don't. I'm not sure if that means Clara wasn't there, or that they were just too young to remember.

Wednesday, March 16, 2011

During our usual car ride to the grocery store, Clara says, "There is a funny thing about my television." I ask what the funny thing is.

"It turns on by itself, in the middle of the night," she tells me.

Really? When we get back to her apartment after shopping, I check out the TV and remote to see if I can find the problem. I see the TV has an alarm that's set for 2:00 a.m. We try to locate the instructions to the television, but they're nowhere to be found. I'm sure at one point Clara impatiently pushed the buttons on the remote without knowing what she was doing and somehow turned on the alarm.

I try to navigate the remote screens without the instructions, but can't figure out how to turn off the alarm. She turns to me and says, "Let it go." She has said this to me before; it's almost as if she uses these words to calm herself. Her aged body becomes relaxed and she looks at me from her blue-and-white-striped chair as if she were an angel.

I tell Clara we can't shop the next week because I will be away on college visits with my oldest daughter. Clara has strong opinions about where my daughter Margie should go to college. The University of Minnesota is the only option because of cost, according to Clara. She can't understand why Margie wants to go away, anyway, and why we are even considering it. I feel that I let Clara's opinions bother me, and at times, I ask myself if I'm becoming too absorbed with Clara. I think about Clara often, even when I'm not with her. My daughters tell me that I talk more about Clara than I do about them. I wonder if they're right.

Wednesday, March 30, 2011

My daughter and I are visiting college campuses, but I can't help but think of Clara and wonder if she's doing okay. I call from North Dakota to check on her. She doesn't answer her phone and I get nervous. I try several more times over the next hour during our stops through the town of Crookston. Margie wants to look at several schools out west for their preveterinary emphasis—large animals. I cannot get a hold of Clara and call the JFCS. They tell me they'll contact the police and ask if an officer can go out and check on her.

I later find out that Clara is fine; she just couldn't hear the phone. It seems to me that someone should be checking in with Clara. *Am I the only one doing this?*

Monday, April 4, 2011

The week after Margie and I get back from our campus visits, Clara calls me a few days before our next shopping day and asks if we can go early on Wednesday because she needs to go to a local community center and have an accountant do her taxes. Apparently, the center offers a tax preparation service during tax season. I'm familiar with the community center because I used to live in the neighborhood where the building is. I tell Clara I will get her at 8:30 a.m.

Wednesday, April 6, 2011

I pick Clara up at 8:30. In the car, Clara complains that her TV is still going on in the middle of the night, and she has to get up to turn it off. I ask her if she wants me to check it again. She says no. I drop her off at the front door of the community center before parking the car.

I haven't been inside the building in many years. I walk down the hall and find Clara sitting in what looks like the waiting area of a doctor's office. A clerk is sitting at a small desk with a sign-in sheet, and I check to make sure Clara has signed in. There is a diverse group of people waiting: elderly, single people, and middle-aged couples. I sit in an open seat next to Clara and watch her fill out a three-page form that she apparently needs to present to the accountants.

The meeting room with accountants is across the hallway from our sitting area. There are several people already in there having their taxes done. After Clara completes her form, I ask her about her week. She tells me about the sales that are happening at the grocery stores. We discuss where we will shop after she gets her taxes done today.

I look across the hall and see a woman being turned away by one of the accountants. She is being told that she needs to have her Social Security card to have her taxes completed. I warily look at Clara and ask her if she has her card. She tells me no. I go over to the clerk sitting at the desk and ask about the need for the Social Security card. She confirms that yes, Clara needs her Social Security card. I go back and try to explain this to Clara. But she brushes it off, saying she does not need the card.

I'm a bit concerned and press her more, asking her where her card is and suggesting that maybe I should go get it. Clara either can't hear me or is choosing to ignore me. I'm anxious; what if we sit here all morning and they turn her away for not having her card? I know she will be angry. My pleas to Clara about her card become embarrassing, since I have to shout for her to hear me. Everyone can hear me talking to her about the card. So I stop talking and we just wait.

The clerk at the desk seems frazzled. Handling all the people waiting to meet with the accountants looks to be too much work for one person. Her job is to check people in and call on each one when it is that person's turn to see an accountant. She calls out names and directs the individuals into the meeting room. There is one problem, though: she forgets to cross the names off the list and she keeps repeating the same names over and over.

And things are even more complicated than that. One woman has been waiting a long time and is breathing from an oxygen tank. Her daughter realizes she is running out of oxygen and asks the clerk if she can have her mother go next in line. The clerk stands up and announces, "There is a woman waiting who is running out of oxygen. Would anyone let her go before them?" No one says yes. She asks a couple more times, but no one will allow it.

I approach the clerk and strike up a conversation. Really, I want to see if I can help her. She tells me that hers is a volunteer position. I really like this clerk, and without thinking, I begin to help her cross the names off the list. I also suggest to the clerk that, instead of making the woman with oxygen wait for her turn, that she should simply call the woman's name next, and no one will be the wiser.

As we wait, I look down the hall and I am surprised to see my daughter's preschool teachers, Patti and Gail. I call out to get their attention. It's been ten years since my youngest attended preschool. Patti tells me that they are in the building to attend a meeting.

Clara and Patti know one another because Clara had volunteered at the preschool several years ago, as I saw in the picture she showed me when we were looking through her photo album. Both Patti and Clara recognize each other right away. Patti has a big smile on her face and is happy to see both of us. She asks what we're doing together. I tell her that I'm Clara's volunteer. Clara says nothing, but nods to Patti politely. She has a look of indifference on her face.

After Patti leaves, Clara tells me about a time when

she volunteered on a field trip with the class. According to Clara, while she (Clara) accompanied the class on a field trip to an apple orchard, she (Clara) gave an apple to one of the students. Patti stopped her, took the apple away, and said that she was not allowed to do that. Clara was not happy with Patti.

As Clara relates the story to me, I want to defend Patti; surely she had a good reason to tell Clara not to share apples with the young children. However, I know better than to argue with Clara. It's best to follow her suggestion and just "let it go."

Clara's name is finally called for her tax meeting. She marches into the room and sits down. I stay in the waiting area and speak with the woman volunteer. I'm still worried about the Social Security card and if Clara has forgotten something else. I don't want to have to go through the whole process of coming back here and waiting again.

Fifteen minutes pass. Things must be going all right, because Clara hasn't come out of the room yet. It must be the Clara charm. Or maybe they are afraid to upset her, like I am.

While she is getting her taxes done, I stay busy helping the clerk. Tax preparation time is going to end by two o'clock. At noon, they have to start turning people away. The current list of customers will take them to two. Clara finally comes out after about an hour. All her taxes are filed and done. She is extremely happy because it was all done for FREE!

Wednesday, April 20, 2011

We are driving in the car on the way home from our usual shopping adventure and Clara is complaining about her TV again. I ask her if she has found the instructions for me to look at. She says that she has not. Clara then asks if I sew. As usual, I'm interested in why she asks. I answer, "Yes, I do. Why do you ask?"

"Oh, no reason," she says in her strange, polite voice. She has the look on her face and tone in her voice that means she wants something.

"Do you have something for me to sew?" I ask, a smile spreading from the corners of my lips, since I am pretty sure I know the answer.

Clara responds, "Well, maybe; but I don't want you to have to go out of your way to do it."

"What do you need sewn?" I ask.

"A robe," she says. I remember seeing it. It was probably soft and plush when Clara first bought it decades ago. Now the fabric is worn thin, and the belt going around the robe has worn down to near nothing.

"Sure. I can do that," I tell her.

Once we get back to her apartment, she hands me what looks like a pile of old rags. There are two full-length cotton polyester robes with tie-around belts. They are pilling, raggedy, and have a distinct old-person's odor. They look like they have been worn every day for the past thirty years. The dark and yellow stains on them gross me out the most.

I reluctantly take the robes. I can't help but think of her boots that I had to duct tape. I figure if she is okay with the duct tape on the boots, she'll be okay with me sewing up her robes, even though I'm probably not the best seamstress.

When I get home, I tell my neighbor Jan about it. She says I should wash them. I don't even want them in my washing machine. I think I would have to replace the washer if I did that, since doing a load of laundry after washing the robes would gross me out. *How terrible of a thought is that?* I don't wash them, but try my best to repair them.

Margie and I drop the robes off to Clara in the middle of the week. Clara is happy.

Wednesday, April 27, 2011

Each week it's the same thing: Clara complains about her TV. She tells me that she read the writing on the back of the remote and it notes something about interference. She keeps making nasty comments about the interference, thinking this is the problem. I think she is blaming the problem with the TV on the remote that I got her. However, she doesn't want to tell me directly.

She complains about the interference, as well as the television turning on at 2:00 a.m. She feels the TV doesn't work as well as it used to. Her channels are fuzzy and blurred, she says. I try everything to correct the problem. Clara's life is her TV, and it is driving me crazy having to listen to her complaints about all of the problems with it.

I can't take the complaining anymore, so I go back to the store and buy a different brand of remote, which is exactly what I was trying to avoid in the first place. As I am programming the new remote, she pulls out three old ones from the drawer of her living room side table. I tell her that I called the store regarding those styles of remote before, and that they had quoted me a higher price when

I asked them what they had in stock. Knowing she is frugal, I was trying to save her some money. This new one was under $20.00, but still she complains. Clara comments that the store quoted me a higher price because they didn't want me to know they had cheaper remotes. According to Clara, it's conspiracy.

I program her new remote and cross my fingers.

The remote works fine, she later tells me, but the TV continues to turn on in the middle of the night. Clara continues to get up each night and turn it off.

Wednesday, May 4, 2011

When I pick up Clara, she tells me she wants to go to three different stores. I can't help but feel like she continuously adds more to her list the more we shop together.

Each time she gives me the list of stores, I map out in my head the quickest and most efficient route. Today, first we go to Aldi for tomatoes and zucchini. Our next stop is Walgreens for $3.00 prunes. Apparently, this is a good price for prunes. Several of our shopping sprees have included searches for sales on prunes.

At Cub Foods, she uses a pushcart, not her usual scooter. The Breyers ice cream that she likes is on sale today. After a few minutes of analyzing her options, she selects two cartons: vanilla-chocolate-strawberry and homemade vanilla. At the checkout counter, she scrutinizes her receipt—as she always does—and finds that they charged her for three ice creams instead of two.

Off to the customer service desk we go to wait in line for money back on the extra ice cream. I can't help to think of all the customers who don't check their receipts and overpay, myself included. I rarely check mine. However, since I have been shopping with Clara, I have started to look over my receipts.

Our last stop for the day is Byerly's. Clara stops at the bank there and makes her deposit with cash back. She always cuts in line and sits at the desk. The teller just goes right ahead and helps Clara, regardless of whether others have been waiting longer. I think Clara expects it. I'm not sure why, but it bothers me that she has these expectations.

By now, Clara is tired and doesn't want to walk to the bakery, but she wants her usual bread. She gives me cash and asks me to get her the Jewish challah bread. I know the routine by now: sliced and double bagged. I find out that the price for challah has gone up ninety-eight cents and Clara has to give me another dollar. She is disgusted about the price increase. After I pay, I return to her the two cents in change. She counts it to make sure it is two cents. Clara says thank you. She always does.

Wednesday, May 11, 2011

In the car, Clara tells me about a neighbor who used to
live next door to her in the building. Her name is Valerie
and she is a nurse. Valerie moved away to be closer to her
work, but while she lived next door to Clara, she would
take Clara shopping, run errands for her, and help Clara
with cleaning and other things around her apartment. It
sounds as if Valerie did a lot for Clara. Valerie also had
a dog that Clara really liked. However, Clara was upset
when Valerie's dog peed on her rug. According to Clara,
the dog peed everywhere, including in Clara's apartment,
because it had a bladder infection. There is some bitterness
in Clara's voice when she tells me this. I wonder what
that is all about.

I try to ask questions, but as usual, Clara only tells
me what she wants me to know. When she does share
things with me about her past, she always tells me that it is
private and not to be repeated.

We are back at Clara's after our usual grocery shopping
and I notice one of the robes that I recently stitched up

59

on the floor in a lump. I pick it up for her and put it on a chair. I think it's funny how I am starting to know Clara so well, and that I'm getting more comfortable doing things like this for her.

She asks me to take some of her old clothes and donate them. I am hoping she means her robes—I can still smell the stink of the one I draped across the chair. Despite how smelly I imagine all of her clothes are, I think, *Hey, no problem; I can handle bringing her things to be donated.* After all, she needs to get rid of some of her old stuff.

Once we put her groceries away, she says in her commanding voice from her chair, "In there," and points to the bedroom. I see three grocery bags on the floor of the bedroom. As I step closer, I realize there is a layer of dust piled on the stack of clothes in each bag. Does the dust ever go away? I cough as I carry them out.

A fog of dust floats everywhere as I carry the bags across the apartment and down to my car. I can't stop sneezing. This is not new dust, but dust that has been sitting around for years, maybe even decades. I have no idea how long the bags have been sitting or how old the clothes are, but from the polyester and styles, I would guess they're from the 1960s or '70s.

I get home and toss the bags in the driveway. I know I have to go through them before I donate anything. More importantly, I need to put them in fresher bags. As I go through the clothing, I find what looks like a pile of rags. There are old slips, old underwear with stains, polyester pants and shirts, stained slippers, worn-out shoes, and so on. *Ugh!* I am disgusted. I sort through and decide to toss a few items. I know how Clara is, and the thought of throwing away any of her things makes me feel bad. However, I know that no one will want these things. I put together a few bags for donation.

I'm up late and like on most nights, I can't sleep well, as thoughts flood my mind, preventing me from dozing off. I'm thinking of Valerie. I would like to talk with her.

Wednesday, May 18, 2011

I would like to have some pictures of Clara shopping, so I take a few using my phone as we make our way around the store. Our experience together isn't something I want to forget. Unfortunately, I forget to save the pictures after I take them.

She asks me to get her a particular brand of orange juice that is on sale. I look, but can't find the juice she wants. I only see grapefruit juice on sale. I go to tell Clara, but can't find her. After a while searching, I find her with a customer who is helping to get the juice she wants. The orange juice is in a different location than the grapefruit juice I had found. Instead of having all the juice selections together, the store has them spread out in four different locations. I am so frustrated.

Even though Clara has found the juice she wants, it is not marked as on sale. I've learned that even though things are not marked as on sale, they can still come up as being on sale at the register. I guess and tell Clara the orange juice isn't on sale. Of course, she proves me wrong a few minutes later when we check with the store clerk.

Sometimes, I wonder if I am the one putting up with her, or if she is the one putting up with me.

Clara still hasn't bought toilet paper since we began shopping. I am a bit concerned. She will only buy the singlewide rolls when they are on sale. When I bring it up, she tells me again that the double rolls don't fit on her toilet paper holder.

Clara and I have been shopping together for five months, and the fish department clerk knows us by now. Earlier today when he saw that I couldn't find her, he said, "She got away from you again." It's as if I am shopping with my grandma who doesn't trust anyone to do anything for her. I have often wondered if Clara prefers having only one helper, so she can readily blame one person, instead of having more than one so she's forced to figure out who's at fault. I feel bad for thinking like this, but I just can't help it.

Last week, when I couldn't take her shopping, she simply didn't go. However, she needed milk, and so she asked her cousin Joy to bring her some. Am I the only one allowed to go shopping?

Wednesday, May 25, 2011

We go to Rainbow today and Clara chooses two large
pieces of lake trout. Clara has also added something
new to her list: Sara Lee carrot cake. Before I know it,
I lose her in the grocery store . . . again. She scoots off
so quickly. I blink my eyes and she's gone. She can't
remember that the bread is near the vegetables, so she
drives her scooter back to the bakery area that we already
passed earlier. I try to tell her, but she either can't hear
me, or chooses not to listen to me. She still refuses to
wear a hearing aid.

I use my phone to take a couple more photos of Clara
shopping. I tell her that I am taking them. She is okay
with it, but wants to know why. I tell her that I want
to remember our time together. I recognized early on
that our experience and relationship is unique; I want to
remember everything we have done and will do together.
I have begun to journal about my time with Clara, too,
and I would like pictures to go along with it. Last week, I
forgot to save the pictures; this time I save them.

On our ride home, Clara tells me that she used to go to the Nankin, a Chinese restaurant that closed its doors in the 1980s. I'm pleasantly surprised. "My family used to own that restaurant," I tell her.

As Clara and I move on our journey together, I find that we have several interconnections. At times when she's mentioned her relatives, she's brought up names that are in my family, too, and I wonder if we are somehow related by marriage. Then there are the preschool and Nankin connections. *Does Clara realize it?*

Just as when I bring up most things, when I mention my family owning the Nankin, she simply gives a slight "Hmm" and continues on with her story, as if she doesn't care that my family had owned one of her favorite restaurants, and that in my younger years I could have easily been her server there. She dismisses the notion and continues talking.

"—We would walk past the long line of waiting customers and be seated, over everyone else," she tells me. She is proud of the fact that the friend she was with at the time seemed so important that he got them a table ahead of everyone else. Likely, he was a friend of my grandfather.

It's funny how sometimes Clara tells me a story out of the blue. Today she also tells me the story of when she managed a Dayton's department store. I can't help but think how terrified I would have been to work for her. She tells me that one time, a customer tried to return a dress that smelled terrible. The clerk who was working at the time got Clara involved. Clara asked the customer where the dress had been, and the lady said, "To lay my Mom out." Can you imagine buying a dress and putting your deceased mother in it before returning it? Clara would not let the woman return the dress, and she instructed all other employees in the store not to take back the dress if the woman tried to return it again. Clara then tells me about Dayton's old policy on returned items: the customer was always right, no questions asked. I have a feeling that Clara didn't follow those instructions well.

When we get back to Clara's apartment, she goes quickly to her TV and turns it on. *The Oprah Winfrey Show* finale is on, and Clara is having a difficult time hearing it. I adjust the volume so she can hear. Maria Shriver is on the show and Clara comments that it's interesting that Oprah introduces her as Maria Shriver, and not Maria Schwarzenegger. I tell Clara that Maria Shriver never went by Schwarzenegger. I get the irked look from Clara, and she brushes off my comment as if I have no idea what I'm talking about. I want to make my point and disagree with her, but instead I let it go.

I can see that in some ways, Clara and I are alike. We both like to be right. I've learned from volunteering with her, that sometimes it doesn't pay to press too hard. Maybe I'm learning to be more patient from spending time with her.

Clara tells me that she continues to get up at night and turn off her TV, and that she has difficulties with the remote. She must still be hitting a wrong button or something, but I'm not so sure. We've already bought her two new remotes, as well as new batteries. Before I leave, she tells me that the television now turns on at random times, not just at night. *Ugh!* I feel that this isn't just Clara's problem, but mine, too. I've done all I can to figure out how to fix this, and nothing I've done has helped. In fact, it seems as if things are getting worse. Is there something wrong with the TV or remote, or is the problem with Clara? This is so frustrating for me. I'm not alone, though; I can see that Clara is frustrated, too.

Wednesday, June 1, 2011

Clara is crabby today—more so than usual, which is a little disturbing. She even apologizes about it afterward. She is obviously distracted, but until she starts complaining about her wrist, I don't know what it's all about. She says it has been hurting for over a week. I offer to take her to the doctor to get it looked at, but she tells me no.

She will only allow her old neighbor Valerie to look at it. For what I am to shopping, Valerie is apparently to any medical issues. I take Clara to get her blood work done today and she doesn't even ask the nurse to look at her wrist.

After we finish with her appointment, we go shopping and then back to her apartment. Her TV is still going on by itself at 2:00 a.m. She continues to have difficulty working the remote and claims that this newer one doesn't work, either. I see that she periodically pushes the video button, and all she needs to do is push the TV button in order to fix the problem. I have shown her this several times before. The nails on her fingers are long, and each time she pushes a button, her fingernail accidentally depresses the video button. I try to explain this to her again, but she doesn't buy my reasoning, and brushes me off with an annoyed look on her face. However, I see her do it all the time. Oh, well.

I sit and briefly talk with Clara today. She tells me that years ago she ran into John McEnroe at Donaldson's, and she had gotten his autograph. *I wonder what John McEnroe was doing at Donaldson's?* Clara loves tennis, and tells me that she watches Wimbledon every year.

Before I leave Clara's apartment, she makes a small comment that she is having a hard time making decisions. Apparently, this has been getting worse. I can't help but worry about her being home alone.

I arrive home and find a bag of Clara's clothes still in my garage. I must have forgotten to donate it with the other bag a couple weeks ago. I make a mental note to remind myself to take care of it.

This week I have been hearing a strange chirping from the top of one of our trees in the backyard. I spend some time trying to figure it out, but I can't identify what kind of bird it is. I even ask the neighbors to listen and see if they can recognize the birdcall. In the evening, my youngest daughter looks out the window in our backyard and says, "Mom, look! There is a baby bunny in the yard."

I look out the window and know right away that it is not a bunny. I go out to investigate. It looks like a baby squirrel to me, obviously in distress, rolling around and not getting anywhere. It is also making that chirping noise I have been hearing. I look for the squirrel's mother to see if she is going to come for the baby. There is no mom— and no other baby squirrels—in sight.

We live in a wooded area and this kind of thing happens quite often in our neighborhood. I consider myself part of the neighborhood distressed wildlife (and nonwildlife) animal club, because I always happen upon suffering or lost animals and feel the need to help them. I quickly get a plastic bin from the basement and poke holes in the top lid. I make my usual call to our local Animal Humane Society. They're about to close, and I'm going to have to care for the squirrel overnight. This is not a surprise—it's the case most of the time when I rescue stray or wild animals. They tell me to keep it warm, since baby squirrels don't produce any body heat. I give the squirrel a small part of an apple. The squirrel chews on it; it's very hungry. Its eyes are barely open.

The squirrel has to stay in the garage overnight. I set the plastic bin on a chair, and put a heating pad against the side. I also put a lamp over the top for extra heat, and wrap Clara's clothes from the forgotten bag in the garage around the plastic bin. I put one of Clara's shirts inside the bin for the baby to sleep on. Clara's clothes finally come in handy! The baby squirrel crawls over to the side of the box where the heat is, and curls up in Clara's clothes.

I decide I need to give him some liquids, too. I find a syringe designed for measuring medicine and put a tiny bit of water in it. I put it up against the squirrel's mouth and he begins to suck. I slowly squirt the water. I'm too fast at first, I guess, because the baby gags. I spend the rest of the night checking on the baby squirrel to make sure he is okay and giving him water. In the morning, I check the Internet and find that a baby squirrel can have Pedialyte. I quickly run to the store, buy a bottle of Pedialyte, and return home to give him some. I wear a glove and pet him. He seems to purr.

I bring the squirrel to the Animal Humane Society and they tell me baby squirrels are tame until they leave the nest, and they do not leave the nest until they are fully grown. Mothers never leave their babies, so something must have happened to the mother. The squirrel will be fine in their hands. The funny thing is, about a week before I found the squirrel, I had commented to one of my daughters, "Why don't we ever see baby squirrels?" Well, I now have my answer.

I use the same plastic bin a few weeks later for a baby pheasant I find in the street. I think an owl must have plucked him from a nest and dropped him there. I do not have to keep him overnight, though! His stay with me is short.

Tuesday, June 7, 2011

Fire!

My husband, Ted, calls to tell me that he heard on the radio that there's a fire in Clara's building. I first try to call Clara, but receive no answer. I begin frantically searching for my information sheet on Clara. It has her emergency contact number on it. I can't find this sheet of paper anywhere. My saved email from Allison, Clara's social worker, is gone, too. *That's weird! Where has everything gone?* I call Beverly at the Jewish Family and Children's Service. It is the Jewish holiday of Shavuot, and their offices are closed.

I next get a call from the Red Cross. They tell me that Clara has asked them to call me. I am starting to worry about Clara's dependence on me. The Red Cross tells me that Clara is fine. Even though I have no idea what I will do with Clara, I tell the Red Cross that I will come and pick her up. *What am I going to do with her?*

Ted arrives home and I quickly leave with his car. I hope that I can get to Clara easily. I am afraid of what I will find at Clara's building.

The street in front of Clara's building is blocked off. However, since I am there to pick up someone who lives in the building, the police let me through the barricade. City buses are parked along the streets, and the residents of the building are sitting on the buses to stay cool. It is hot and the temperature is 101 degrees.

True to form, Clara is not on the bus. No one knows where she is. We finally figure out that someone has taken her to a bathroom across the street. When I meet up with her, she is in her pink housecoat and slippers, looking worn and tired. However, she is surprisingly calm and does not seem rattled by what is happening around her. She tells me that a firefighter axed down her door, picked her up, threw her over his shoulder, and carried her down the stairwell to safety. The entire time, she was hitting and screaming at him that he was hurting her. Her body is obviously frail, and I have a feeling that anything anyone might do to her would hurt.

I speak to the Red Cross officials and they aren't sure if Clara will be able to get back in her apartment later. A nice woman from the Red Cross went into Clara's apartment after the building had been cleared by the fire department and picked up some of Clara's things: purse, watch, ring, medication, and some clothing. The Red Cross volunteers and I discuss several options for Clara. We decide that I will temporarily take her—just for dinner—and then return back to the building for further instructions. I decide to take Clara to dinner at Byerly's in her housecoat and slippers.

At dinner, Clara tells me she sat on that bus from 1:00 until 5:30 p.m. when I showed up—less the time for the bathroom visit. She tells me that the steps to get to the area where the bathroom was were so steep that she had to crawl up them. I can't quite picture what Clara is talking about; however, envisioning Clara crawling up stairs in her pink housecoat and slippers makes me very sad. She tells me that the Red Cross had provided her with several bottles of water—hence, her need to use the bathroom.

I tell her that I wish I had my camera to take a picture of her in her housecoat and slippers at Byerly's. She says, "I would shoot you if you took a picture of me like this." At first, I laugh at her wisecrack; it fits her edgy personality. But I almost immediately wonder if her comment just confirms my feeling that if I ever did anything to upset her, she would get really mad at me. I ask if she's gone out in her housecoat before. This time, *she* laughs. I'm trying to make light of the situation.

While Clara eats, my phone rings. It's my mom. She knows that I'm with Clara at Byerly's because I had called her earlier to tell her about the fire and what was going on. My mom and I are good friends and talk several times a day. She is familiar with my relationship with Clara. And just as Ted has, she expresses her concerns about me taking on extra things—like Clara. My mom likes to joke that by caring for Clara, I'm getting practice for when she is old so that I can take care of her.

My mom tells me that she is at Byerly's, too. She's accidently left her purse at home, and needs money for her groceries and dinner. I tell her to come to the restaurant and I will give her the money she needs. I am interested to see what Clara's reaction will be. Knowing Clara's personality, I anticipate some kind of scrutiny for what we are doing. My mom stops by and I introduce her to Clara. They cordially shake hands, and my mom sits next to me as Clara tells her about the fire. It's interesting seeing the two of them talk. After the conversation, I hand my mom money so she can pay for her groceries. Out of the corner of my eye, I can see a look of disapproval on Clara's face. She does not say anything; however, I know what she's thinking: *her mom is being irresponsible.*

I still can't get a hold of anyone at the JFCS. I don't know exactly what my responsibilities are with Clara, and am worried I'm overextending them. I'm not sure what I'm going to do with Clara.

When I rushed out of my house to get to Clara, I left with Ted's car so quickly that he didn't get a chance to take his work files out of the car. Clara and I have to drive to my house to give Ted his work. Clara asks me if Ted brings work home a lot. I tell her that he does. From what Clara has told me about herself, I know that she has a strong work ethic. She has no problem with me wanting to bring Ted his work. We arrive in my driveway and I glance over at Clara seated next to me in the passenger's seat. I see her fixing her hair and housecoat. How cute it is that she's trying to look presentable. I call Ted from the driveway and he comes out to the car. I get out of the driver's seat and he reaches in and shakes Clara's hand.

Ted tells her he is sorry to hear about the fire. Clara seems happy to meet him.

Clara and I drive back to her building to meet with the Red Cross volunteers. They tell me that they haven't found anyone available to take Clara in. The fire is proving to be a big turning point for me, as it's the first time I realize Clara really does not have a lot of support and is relying on me more and more. This scares me a lot. Hanging in her apartment, she has a poster-sized photo of a family reunion with well over one hundred relatives in it. *Where is everyone?* I'm not sure I understand it.

The Red Cross volunteers look to me to take responsibility for Clara. I explain the situation to them; I am a volunteer with the JFCS and not related to Clara. I tell them I cannot get a hold of the JFCS to find out exactly what to do with Clara because the JFCS is closed for a holiday. I'm not sure if I'm allowed to take Clara to my house and I'm not going to chance it; what if something happens to her at my house? The Red Cross determines it's best that Clara be placed in a motel.

I fill out the necessary paperwork. The Red Cross has made arrangements for Clara to stay at a motel about ten minutes from her apartment. I have to admit I'm concerned about Clara being alone in a motel, but what can I do? It seems like the only viable option right now. Clara is fine with it, too. The Red Cross is paying; and she is willing to go wherever they put her.

I drop Clara off at the door to the motel and park the car. Once inside, I realize that I need to fill out more paperwork for Clara. As I do this, I hear Clara in her huffy voice say to the clerk, "If the room is too far down the hallway, I will shoot you." The clerk is laughing. But Clara isn't.

I help Clara settle into a comfortable handicap-accessible room halfway down the main hallway. In her room I put a chair in front of the television for her to sit in. *At least this TV won't go on in the middle of the night.* I've known Clara for about six months and have listened to her talk about Valerie, but I have yet to talk to her myself. I would have loved to talk to Valerie today.

Wednesday, June 8, 2011

The day after the fire, I'm at the motel to meet with Clara to figure out a plan for her. I have my truck with me, but I need the smaller car, knowing that I may have to drive Clara around today. Margie is out for breakfast with Ted's mom nearby, and I call her to meet me at the motel so that we can switch cars.

I try calling Clara from the lobby, but she doesn't answer. I ask the clerk if he has seen or heard from her, and he says she came out earlier this morning for breakfast. I'm glad to hear she's eating. After several calls, she still doesn't answer her phone.

The clerk walks Margie and me down the hall to Clara's room. I knock on the door as loudly as I can, and Clara opens the door. Thank goodness she's all right. Clara invites Margie and me into her room. Clara asks Margie about her college visits, and then proceeds to tell us that she liked the continental breakfast at the motel, but they ran out of milk.

Due to the fact that the fire alarm system in her building is not fixed yet, Clara won't be able to go back to her apartment, so we need to arrange at least another night at the motel. The JFCS is still closed because of the holiday. In order for Clara to stay additional days at the motel, she has to check out, get reapproved by the Red Cross, then check back in with the new paperwork. The front desk manager at the motel is understanding and says Clara can have the same room when she returns.

We drive downtown to the Red Cross; Clara wants to stay in the car because she's too tired to walk. I think the last couple of days have worn her out. I go in, register, and wait for a representative to meet with me. Clara's name is called. I sit with the representative to reapply for another night at the motel. The representative decides they will approve two more nights for Clara, just in case she can't get back into her apartment for a couple of days. That way I won't have to bring Clara back downtown for more paperwork. The representative walks with me out to my car so Clara can sign the paperwork.

After we settle things with the Red Cross, I take Clara to Byerly's, the bank, and then to Rainbow. At Rainbow, her scooter runs out of power. One of the workers has to drive a charged scooter to the aisle where we are. I'm glad *he* did it and not me; I would have been too embarrassed driving the scooter around. I think it's interesting, with all that is going on—the fire and being displaced from her apartment—that Clara's only real concern seems to be whether she will be able to use her coupon for six boxes of Total cereal and save $9.00. Clara has a minirefrigerator in her motel room, so she gets some tomatoes, bread, bananas, one orange, and milk. She is not happy that the orange costs $1.04.

After all of the time I've spent wondering if Valerie would think it's strange that I contact her, it is Valerie who contacts me first.

Valerie has somehow gotten my number and calls me. Her voice is warm and caring. I also sense sadness and something unresolved. I picture Valerie young, strong, and very pretty. She's been trying to call Clara at the motel so she can talk to her, but Clara must not have heard the phone in her motel room. She never answered Valerie's call. Valerie wants Clara to stay with her instead of at the motel. She tells me to have Clara contact her. This is interesting; her old neighbor is willing to take her in. Does she know Clara well?

I tell Clara about my conversation with Valerie. Clara expresses that she doesn't want to go stay with Valerie. She says, "I don't want to get back with Valerie anymore." I can't understand why Clara seems so estranged from Valerie. All she ever mentions about Valerie are good things. Clara talks about how much she loved Valerie's dog and about how much Valerie did for her.

In the car, Clara tells me about an accident on a city bus that happened many years ago. She had been standing at the front of the city bus, waiting to get off, and the driver slammed on his brakes. According to the driver, a person stepped in front of the bus and he had to do it. Clara flew forward and hit her head on the coin machine, which gave her a concussion and other injuries. She was in the hospital for weeks and out of work for months. The only person who came to visit her in the hospital was one coworker. Again, I start to get a woozy feeling, knowing how few people there are in Clara's life. Clara said the coworker could hardly recognize her because she was so bruised and swollen. Clara had been in her sixties, thirty years before I knew she existed.

I am quiet and tired when I get Clara back to the motel. I check her in and bring her back to her same room. I remind her how to use the TV. I set up a chair again for her between the two beds. I can't help but feel sorry for her, and wonder if I'm doing the right thing. Before I leave, I stop and stare at her sitting in the chair, her back to me and the TV on.

Thursday, June 9, 2011

I call Valerie. It's been a couple of days since the fire; she feels bad about not being there for Clara and hopes to make amends with her. I can tell she feels awful about losing touch with Clara. Valerie tells me that she lived next to Clara for five years. She helped with shopping and anything else Clara needed. She moved out a year before I met Clara. Valerie moved to be closer to her nursing job. It is twenty-two miles away from Clara's building. After she moved, she continued to help Clara for a while, but then lost contact with her.

The last time Valerie helped Clara, Clara had asked Valerie to pick up a peach and Valerie accidently selected a nectarine. Valerie told Clara that she had simply made a mistake and grabbed the wrong fruit. Clara was mad and accused Valerie of doing it on purpose. They disagreed about it. After that, Clara wouldn't return Valerie's phone calls. It took something as simple as a piece of fruit to end things.

Valerie is planning to visit Clara next Sunday. She offers to take her to the store, too, but Clara refuses because she wants to go with me on Saturday. I was hoping for the break. I guess it's not going to happen.

Since the first day I met Clara, she has had long hairs on her chin. They have continued to grow over the past months. I would love to take her to electrolysis. However, I know Clara will never pay for anything like that. She plays with the hairs all the time—grabs them and pulls down as a man with a beard would. Today, Clara expressed to me that she needs a new electric razor to shave the hair off her chin. I am very surprised that she is conscious of it. I'm not sure why it surprises me; I guess I thought she didn't pay it much attention.

Clara is just going with the flow with this whole fire displacement situation. I expect her to be angry, but she isn't uptight whatsoever about being stuck in a motel. This isn't the Clara I've come to know the past six months. If I had to guess before all this happened what she would be like, I'd say she'd be irritated and outspoken about it. However, at times, she surprises me. Maybe it's the ease of the TV working at the motel, with no remote problems or having to get up to turn off the TV at 2:00 a.m.

We finally get the okay for Clara to return to her apartment. Upon entering, I immediately react to the smell of smoke and chemicals in the lobby—it's nasty! It must be the cleaning agents. I'm sensitive to chemicals and smoke. The foul odor is so unbearable that I want to leave, but I can't because I need to help Clara back to her apartment.

Surprisingly, her place itself doesn't smell very smoky. It just smells of the usual stale air. There is an extra layer of dust on top of the dust that was already there before the fire. Her door doesn't work, either, due to the fireman axing through the lock and frame in order to rescue Clara. Clara marches right to her chair, sits, and turns on her TV. She wants to know that it works. Thankfully, it does! After dealing with a few days of her displacement, I don't think I could deal with her television not working.

She takes me to her den where she has a sweater lying on a chair and asks if the front border pattern can be removed. It is an edging along the front, and she thinks it can be used for something different. The sweater has holes, but she likes the trim. Not sure what she has in mind with the old thing. I am surprised she is even thinking about this right now. It seems to me there is more to worry about, like getting her place clean after the fire and getting the door fixed. She is acting as if a fire never even happened. Clara must have taken the sweater out to ask me before the fire occurred. I tell her I don't think I can remove the trim without damaging it.

Saturday, June 11, 2011

I'm driving and I look at Clara as she speaks. I sometimes glance at her when she is telling me a story. I am so lost in looking at her that I almost hit the car in front of us. It's like she's a giant animated doll, and I'm a child completely mesmerized with her. I see all of those things that are unattractive about her, such as the hair on her chin, her leathery and aged skin, and eyes lined with heavy bags. At the same time, I look at her knowing she's been alive for more than nine decades, and was once my age. As much as I find myself frustrated with her, I also find myself fascinated by her.

Today is Saturday, not our usual shopping day. Clara and I agreed to change it this week because of the fire. I do the usual routine and drop Clara off at the door before parking the car.

When I enter the grocery store, I can't see her anywhere. She is usually in the fruit and vegetable area—or near there—when I walk into the store, but I can't find her. I am nervous as I search the entire store four times over. *Where can an elderly woman in a scooter be?*

I even go into the liquor store to see if she happened to stop in there. I decide to get the manager and see if he can help me find her. I'm starting to think I've lost my mind.

So many things begin to cross my mind. *Did someone take her?* Right; who is going to take an elderly woman in a scooter? Why am I getting so upset? Clara is a grown woman and can take care of herself. I go so far as to think that my entire volunteer gig never really happened—there is not really a Clara. It's funny, in a time of personal fear and crisis, where our minds will lead us. Even while thinking these things, I know they are crazy notions, but they still insist on coming to me.

The store manager and I finally find her in the canned vegetable aisle. I am relieved but also a bit angry. I want to lecture her as if she were one of my kids who hadn't listened and had run off, but of course I can't. She hasn't done anything wrong. I'm just being myself: panicked.

When we're at the register to check out, I'm nervous about what's going to happen. I know Clara's coupon for eggs is going to expire. Since there are no eggs, she wants a rain check. It is a manufacturer's coupon, so they won't give her the rain check. Clara has an irritated look on her face and she starts to make a fuss about the coupon. Seeing Clara's displeasure, the cashier kindly puts her own name on the coupon so Clara can come back in a week and use the coupon for eggs.

After checking out, Clara inspects her receipt. She is charged incorrectly for the two peaches. How is it that almost every time we go shopping together she is charged incorrectly for something? It makes me wonder how much money I've been overpaying for all these years. I have to take the receipt to the customer service desk. The peaches are mismarked. They are marked $1.49. However, they are actually supposed to be marked $2.49. The manager, knowing Clara quite well by now, is kind enough to give her the lower price for the peaches and pays her back the difference in cash. We escape the store relatively unscathed and I let my worries go as I walk out to the car.

Clara tells me that all her cousins have been talking about the fire in her building. Her comment surprises me, because as far as I know, the only relative she talks to is her cousin Joy. I ask her how she knows they're talking about it. She dismisses my question. A feeling crosses over me that the fire will, in fact, affect my life much longer than it will Clara's.

Her building still smells bad enough that I have to wear a mask to cover my mouth and nose, as I have done a few times before. She has told me that she can't lock her door because of her wrist. I check the door to see if it has been fixed, and I see where the firefighters cracked the edge of her door when they broke in to get her out. I make a mental note to have it checked out. Next, she asks if I can look at the upper shelves in her kitchen cabinet. The shelf with the pots and pans sitting on it has fallen down. The problem is a simple fix, as it is only a broken plastic clip, which I replace with a metal one she already has sitting in the cabinet. Her sliding door to her patio deck won't close, either. I fix it.

She then asks me if I can figure out how to fix her table. She must think I'm able to fix anything. I feel more like a "volunteer handyman" than a "volunteer visitor." Her cabinet in the den must have had something sitting on it for years. Some sort of glue is stuck to it. I, of course, can't fix that one. My eyes scan her apartment, almost as if I were searching for more things to fix. As much as I am intimidated by doing things for Clara, always anticipating a comment or glare, I feel good knowing that I am helping her.

Clara mentions that Valerie is going to visit on Sunday. From the way Clara was talking the previous week, I have to admit I'm surprised. Apparently, she respects Valerie much more than she lets on. She is going to ask Valerie to look at her wrist. Regardless of the grudge Clara holds against Valerie, she still trusts her old neighbor more than she would a doctor.

Wednesday, June 15, 2011

I had taken Clara to the store on Saturday; however, she still wants to do more grocery shopping today.

I go up to her apartment to help her lock her door. She still can't do it because of her wrist and the fact that the door is still broken from the fire. It still smells in the building and I don't have my mask today.

We first go to Byerly's and stop at the bank there. We then begin our shopping. She has me push her in the wheelchair today. She is lighter than I expect.

We go to the meat display and look at all the meats at the counter. She doesn't choose any of the meat. We then go to the prepackaged meats and look at all of those. I use a plastic bag to touch all the meat packages she wants me to hold up and show her. Clara gives me the look, as if she were rolling her eyes without actually showing it. I know she thinks I'm nuts. She chooses a large piece of steak. We then go back to the butcher counter where Clara has the butcher package another piece of beef. After the red meat, we go to the seafood. She feels there isn't enough to choose from and the prices are too high. She shakes her head in disappointment. No seafood today, I guess.

Clara tells me about a woman named Jessica from the county's social services department having visited her. I already know she had visited Clara, because Jessica called me about it, too. Apparently, someone called social services after the fire and told them there was an elderly, at-risk woman staying at the motel. Somehow, social services got my number. Jessica tells me that she had a nice visit with Clara and determined Clara is fine living on her own.

Clara's livelihood *is* her apartment, as is cooking on her own, and, of course, her television. Except for when she needs to go shopping and to doctor appointments, Clara is independent and likes to take care of herself.

Clara next asks to go to Cub Foods. I don't want to take her, but I do. Clara gets a lot of tomatoes because they are on sale. Blueberries are "buy one get one free" with a coupon. I grab a coupon to take advantage of the sale, too. Clara has been looking for a special three-way lightbulb. We finally find one here. She analyzes a single pack with a lightbulb that will last for 2,400 hours and then a two-pack with lightbulbs that will last 1,200 hours each. She grabs the single pack because it's cheaper.

We get to the ice cream cooler, and Breyers is on sale: two cartons for $6.99. I knew there was a reason why she wanted to shop again this week! Clara next wants to look at the kosher meats. She doesn't need any more meat.

What is she thinking? She already has some in the car. I'm trying to rush her because of this. I don't want them to spoil.

Checking out is the usual. She can't hear when the cashier tells her the total, so she doesn't write the check until she can see the total or I shout it to her. Clara seems happy today.

I don't call Clara for the rest of the week. Since March, I'd been calling a couple times a week to check on her. But for some reason—whether it's because I'm busy or need time to myself—I don't pick up the phone.

Wednesday, June 22, 2011

I sort of know what Clara is capable of, regarding her temper. I think I have always assumed it could be bad, but after several months together, I finally see her in action. I take her to Walgreens to get her prescription filled. I drop her off at the door and park the car. I take a call from Jessica at social services. She is going to stop by Clara's this afternoon for another visit. Jessica wants to close the file on Clara.

After the call, I go inside Walgreens and walk toward the pharmacy, where I see Clara at the counter arguing with the clerk. Clara has this frightening look on her face, and is using language that I have not heard her use before. She is upset about something having to do with her thyroid medicine, and she is actually yelling and swearing! My first reaction is to run away as fast as I can. I want to call the JFCS and say, *"I'm done! This woman scares me way too much!"*

I can't believe what I am seeing and hearing, and I try to figure out what the issue is. The same clerk we'd seen the last time we picked up Clara's prescription is trying to explain the issue to Clara. Finally, the pharmacist comes over and tries to calm Clara.

She says, "Clara, we are going to speak to each other rationally. First I am going to talk, and then you can speak." The pharmacist starts to speak and explain, but Clara immediately cuts her off and starts in again. The pharmacist walks away and comes back with a piece of paper. She writes the explanation on the paper. The pharmacist keeps referring to Clara's insurance and Clara keeps yelling that she doesn't have insurance. I finally figure out what the issue is. Clara received a coupon in the mail that allows her a discount on her thyroid medicine. But she can't get the entire prescription all at once. The coupon only allows for a small portion each time, but Clara wants all of her pills at one time at a discount.

I try to tell Clara that the coupon is causing the problem, not Walgreens, but she is so mad at Walgreens and the people working there she won't listen to anyone. Clara is livid, and the scene she's making is crazy! Clara marches out and vows never to go back to Walgreens. She is breathing so heavily and is so excitable that she has drained herself. I'm actually starting to worry for her. What if she simply collapses? I don't know if I can handle something like that right now.

Once we're in the car, I tell her I'm never going to make her mad. I think I'm trying to make her laugh or smile—even just smirk—to break her anger, but she isn't budging. She isn't just mad; she is furious. I'm actually scared of her.

I thought about the story she shared with me regarding her bus accident, and only having one visitor while she was in the hospital. I wonder how she behaved with the hospital staff; I also wonder what it would have been like to work with her in a place of employment. When she was mad at coworkers, did she behave like this? I suspect that many people have been turned off by her behavior throughout her life. She's convinced that people are trying to cheat her. It's a level of paranoia even I never get to. For Clara, it's almost an obsession.

After Walgreens, we go to the grocery store. According to Clara, paper towels are on sale today for $5.98. We get to the paper goods aisle and there is no sign showing the sale price. Shopping with Clara is always like this: she wants the advertised price she has seen in the newspaper, but when we get to the store, the item she wants is not marked correctly. As usual, I go get a clerk. When I come back, she has the coupon in front of her. I ask her why she didn't have the coupon out before I went to look for someone!

It's been a few weeks since the fire, and it still seems to be affecting me more than it does her. I hold my breath or wear a mask when I'm in her building. I'm worried about being afflicted with some horrible disease from the smoke, dust, toxic chemicals, or—most alarming—asbestos. I'm bothered by the fact that she does not even consider getting her apartment cleaned. I wonder if she even remembers the fire, since she never talks about it. It's almost as if it were something that happens all the time, kind of like our shopping.

Wednesday, July 6, 2011

We go to Rainbow, and then to Byerly's. She buys a lot of meat again at Byerly's. I ask if she has eaten the meat from the previous week. She hasn't. I wonder why she buys expensive meats when she is so frugal, so I ask her, and she says she buys these meats out of respect for her father. She uses a Yiddish word that I can't quite hear but it sounds like "saygal." I don't know what she means, but the look on her face (as though I'm clueless) stops me from asking anything more.

In the car, she tells me about her association board meeting that's coming up. The meeting is to discuss the fire. I tell her she should go. She has to know what is going on in her building. She dismisses my comment, so I don't know what she will do. I feel like I should show up to make sure she goes.

I ask if she had friends when she was growing up. She says that there was no one around to play with, only her siblings, and no Jewish children. I wonder if that means they were only allowed to play with the Jewish children, and that's why she didn't have many friends. I ask if she had friends when she moved to the city. She said she had one friend named Betty—"Who was fat," she says. Betty was a good friend. When Betty moved to Chicago, Clara visited her there, and they had a good time.

Clara wants to go to Aldi. We stop there, but she doesn't like the selections and doesn't buy anything. *It was a waste of time to stop.* I think Clara actually thinks the same thing!

Clara is very curious about my relationship with my husband, Ted. She asks if we are spending more time together since two of our kids are away at camp. I tell her I am spending more time with my daughter who is not at camp. Clara finds it strange that I do things with my children. She says her parents never did stuff with her and her siblings. Because she has never been married, nor does she have kids, it seems that she does not quite understand what my life is like.

Clara's television is still having problems. She is convinced the remote is causing interference because the television continues to turn on in the middle of the night. I know it's the timer and not the remote. I can't find the instructions for the television to figure out how to turn off the timer. The TV thing is driving me crazy. When I get a chance, I'm going to search the Internet for instructions about how to properly operate her TV.

I'm so curious about what Clara meant when she used the Yiddish word that sounded like "saygal." I look it up when I get home. I find a Yiddish word that is similar, "seykhl": "common sense." The look on her face must have meant that I should have known the answer because it was common sense.

Wednesday, July 13, 2011

Clara wants to go to Herberger's today to get nightgowns.
On our way, she comments on how well I know my
way around everywhere. I tell her it's because I do a lot
of driving, given all of my kids' activities. I drop her at
the door and park the car. When I get in the store, she
is waiting for me. We grab a cart for her to hold onto
and use for balance. She can only make it through one
department before she has to rest. It takes us a long time
to get to the nightgowns. The aisles are so narrow that we
can hardly move the cart around. She wants a medium-
sized nightgown, and says she doesn't need to try it on.
She seems to know a lot about the styles and brands.

After she selects three nightgowns, we go to the
register. I'm surprised she's even going to buy them.
It's funny; nightgowns were one of the first things she
mentioned she wanted to shop for with me, and it took us
seven months to do it. She waited for a sale, of course.

At the register, she needs her identification to register
her Herberger's account. She has a coupon and a senior
citizen discount. Why else would we be here? She wants

to check the prices before she will buy them. Clara wants the lowest price with all the discounts. The woman at the register is patient with Clara and asks how old she is.

"Almost ninety-three," Clara replies politely. The woman I'd seen screaming at the pharmacist is well gone. It's amazing to me the change I see in her sometimes. One day she's flying off the handle at someone, and the next day she looks like a sweet grandmother.

I turn to Clara, realizing I don't know when her birthday is. "When's your birthday?" I ask.

She gives me a curious look and says, "Do you know your husband's name?" as if her birthday is common knowledge, and I am the only one who doesn't know. I have no idea what her comment really means, and I don't pursue the question.

The cashier tells Clara that she is going to look sexy in her new nightgowns. Clara can't hear her and asks me what the clerk has said. I look around and see customers lined up everywhere. I don't want to repeat the comment, so I say in a loud voice that I know Clara will hear, "THE CASHIER SAID YOU ARE GOING TO LOOK PRETTY IN YOUR NEW NIGHTGOWNS." All the customers laugh because they know the clerk said "sexy."

In true fashion, Clara tells me today is her birthday. I feel terrible that I didn't know. Here we are shopping together on her birthday and we aren't doing anything special—although, after ninety-three birthdays, shopping is special, I suppose. We hug and I fight back my tears.

In the car, I tell Clara what the clerk had really said. Clara responds, "An old, sexy hag," and I smile.

Wednesday, July 20, 2011

I call Clara and she tells me that it's too hot for her to go out, and she does not want to shop today. We agree on Saturday for our next shopping date.

Saturday, July 23, 2011

Clara seems happy. We go to Rainbow and Byerly's.
Clara tells me about her mom passing away from heart
failure at a young age. During the time when her mom
was ill, Clara and her siblings were told by their father
they weren't allowed to say anything that would upset
their mother. Clara often drops these small curiosities
about her younger years as we shop, and then moves on
as if she'd said nothing at all. I find it interesting to hear
about her past, and enjoy listening to her stories.

As per usual, she buys meat and tomatoes today. She
has me put back the tomatoes once she finds a different
kind that is cheaper. This happens so much I don't think
I'm bothered—or surprised—by it anymore.

Wednesday, July 27, 2011

Clara asks if we can go back to a grocery store because she realized she was overcharged for sweet potatoes two weeks ago. In addition, she feels she overpaid for the milk and cottage cheese. With the number of times Clara has found a mistake on her receipts, I again can't help but wonder how much money I've overspent all these years.

We stop at the customer service desk. After several minutes of reviewing the error, they find that, yes, Clara was incorrectly charged for the sweet potatoes. However, the milk and cottage cheese were correct. She gets back sixty cents for the mischarge on the sweet potatoes. I had also bought the same sweet potatoes two weeks ago. However, I don't have my receipt anymore to get my money back. Even if I still had it, I'm not sure I would take the time to bring it back for the sixty cents.

Clara seems determined and focused today. She gets like this whenever she's right about finding a discount that the store missed at checkout. It's almost as if she wants to flaunt her achievement without actually saying anything. Clara grabs a gallon of milk because she has a coupon for free milk. She still has a gallon at home in her refrigerator. She also still has a lot of meat and fruit at home. She chooses more fish.

When we get to the checkout counter, the can of salmon rings up at a different price than she expects. I see that she did not select the can labeled with the price she had seen posted. I have to explain this to her. However, the clerk gives her the price of the cheaper can. I think the clerk just doesn't want to argue about it.

Clara tells me that her housekeeper needs cleaning supplies. Clara decides it would be better to go to the hardware store next week to get these supplies. Why would she want to do this? Maybe she thinks they will be cheaper. The hardware store is farther away. The difference in gas will make it a wash in cost. As usual, I just do whatever Clara wants. I don't want to upset her. Her housekeeper needs supplies.

When we get back to her apartment, she has me check her den closet for rubber gloves. The closet is packed with stuff. I find rubber gloves, but they look ancient and brittle.

Clara is a bit tired today. Her breathing is heavy after walking. Her apartment continues to smell worse each week, and it is no longer from the fire smoke. I'm not sure how to describe it, the kind of stale stink of the air. I am starting to get concerned about the meat in her refrigerator. She is not eating it up quickly enough. I ask her if she ate the meat she bought the previous week. She tells me no. I worry about her getting sick from bad meat.

Wednesday, August 3, 2011

When I call to tell Clara I will be there at 1:00 p.m., she tells me she has a lot to do. Her comment makes me laugh. I compare what she thinks is a lot to what I think is a lot. If she knew exactly what I do each day, she would probably think I'm nuts. Because she's never had children, I'm not sure she really knows what counts as a lot to do. Maybe in her past jobs she was very busy, though. I can't really know what her life before I knew her was like.

Our first stop is for another haircut. She gets the same bowl cut as before, only this time the haircut is $14.00, not $8.00. Clara complains to the cashier that the cost of the cut is too high. I explain to Clara that it was cheaper last time because she had the coupon. Clara is upset, but she lets it go.

Next stop is Herberger's to return one of the nightgowns we bought a few weeks back. Thankfully, the return is uneventful. After we leave Herberger's, we go to the hardware store for cleaning supplies (mop, Lysol, Lime-A-Way, vacuum bags). We then go to the bank at

Byerly's and Rainbow. I tell Clara that the Breyers ice cream is on sale at Cub Foods, and ask her if she wants to go there. She says no. I'm shocked that she is passing up a sale on her favorite ice cream. She must be too tired after all the things we did today.

We are back at Clara's, and she asks me if I listen to what Ted says. She has asked me this before. I think she feels my children may be spoiled because I do too much for them. She tells me that my children should be doing the cooking and cleaning. Times are so different from when she was growing up. She has never had children and doesn't really know what it's like.

She expels gas, and I leave quickly.

Saturday, August 13, 2011

Clara calls me while I am on a family vacation to let me know the road in front of her building will be closed on Wednesday this week, and that I won't be able to pick her up. She wants me to take her shopping on Monday. I tell her I'm going to be out of town until late Monday night and I can't get there on Monday. I can tell she is annoyed that I won't be home in time to take her, but there isn't anything I can do. We settle on the following Wednesday.

Sunday, August 14, 2011

Last night, I had a bad nightmare: I drop Clara off somewhere and forget to pick her up. When I finally do get there, she is so mad that she smacks me. I've always been afraid she's going to get mad at me and blow up. I can sense the volatility in her. She often scares me to the point where I want to call the JFCS and say, "Forget it. I can't handle this anymore."

I feel angry and sad at the same time. I don't want to feel angry with her, but I do sometimes. I am frustrated that she doesn't have any help other than me. She has probably turned everyone away. She can be so difficult, and thinks everyone is trying to cheat her. I'm afraid that if I leave her, she will be alone. I feel this overwhelming obligation to her. I don't know why. I'm a strong person, but I don't understand why I feel afraid of her. Maybe I just don't want to get into an argument with her. It would be embarrassing if either of us had to contact the JFCS and terminate our relationship because we had an argument. Who would even understand this?

Wednesday, August 24, 2011

I have so many emotions regarding my volunteer time with Clara. I'm troubled because it seems that she relies on me more than she should. On the other hand, she does not ask me for much, or the things that she does ask of me are really not that big of a deal.

It's a strange feeling, this inner struggle that I am having. I'm not sure why I'm so bothered by my volunteering with her. I get frustrated when she is angry, and I am irritated when she gets so excessive with her coupons. However, I am happy that she is frugal and can live on her own, and within her means. Other times I enjoy spending time with her. I find Clara funny, and she makes me laugh, especially when *she* laughs. I can't quite figure out how I feel about my time with her.

When I arrive to pick her up there is a truck in the way, and she has to walk to the street to get to my car. She smells terrible! I am having a hard time with this, to say the least. Her apartment also continues to smell and I can't figure out why.

She tells me the whole story about her washer breaking this week and how her cousin Joy took her to purchase a new washer and dryer unit. The entire time she is telling me the story, I'm thinking, Thank goodness I was out of town, and it wasn't me who had to take her to buy the washer and dryer. According to Clara, the salesperson would not give her an exact price during the sales discussion. Clara says he kept using the word "estimate."

Clara did not like the fact that he kept saying "estimate," so she said to the salesperson, "I don't like you." She tells me that in all her years in sales, she had never said that to anyone. I can only imagine how upset she was with the salesperson. Clara says that the salesperson ended up walking away. They found a new salesperson who sold her a machine. Clara complains about the $70.00 to haul away her old machine, and feels the price was too high because, as she tells me, "They sell the machine for scrap metal and get money for it." I feel better knowing that Joy was there to help her. I just don't want to get involved with things like this.

After telling her story, she explains to me she is a numbers person. *Ha! Oh, really? I haven't noticed!* I wonder if she has figured out that I am not a numbers person. I will never tell her that I have dyslexia. If I do tell her, I can only imagine where that conversation would go.

As we talk, I tell her how much I pay for my children's school supplies each year. Clara is shocked. She responds by telling me how the miners provided all the funding for her childhood school. According to Clara, the school had good facilities. She also tells me she went to Hibbing Junior College and then to the University of Minnesota. And back then, they did not have to pay very much for secondary schooling.

Valerie took Clara shopping while I was out of town and bought her flowers. Clara seems happy while she is telling me this.

It's the usual shopping today. The orange juice is on sale. With Clara's coupon, and it being Wednesday—the day they double the coupons—her orange juice costs $1.00. I am still frustrated watching her go around the store without a plan. We go from one side to the next, and back again. It wastes so much time! It's kind of funny that she is a penny pincher, yet she isn't very efficient when it comes to mapping out her grocery shopping escapades. I could get her shopping done in a third of the time.

She has to get a lot of groceries because she hasn't been able to get out for a few days due to the construction in the parking lot. Clara complains about the carrots she bought a couple weeks ago. The bag had been wet when she bought them, and the carrots went bad, forcing her to toss them. I'm sure this made her angry.

She is looking at cod and lake trout, and as usual insists on selecting the fat pieces. The butcher has to hold up every piece of fish several times until she makes a decision. I try to help Clara pick out fish; she just pushes me out of the way. The butcher always seems so annoyed with us. *I can't imagine why.*

At the register, Clara is charged the wrong price for the bag of potatoes. We have to stand in the customer service line for them to check it and give her back the fifty cents they overcharged her. She is so sharp with her calculations and knows exactly when she is charged incorrectly. Clara is charged the wrong price on something almost every week, regardless of what store we visit. It's aggravating. It adds time on to our grocery shopping—waiting for them to check the price and then give her money back. Most people don't check their receipts that closely. If everyone did, the customer service line would be out the door.

I tell Clara I'm annoyed by the fact that the grocery stores have problems with their pricing and computers. She seems to accept it for what it is. We then go to another store for bread and meat. She tells me she needs to return the vacuum bags she got at the hardware store. I'm not surprised.

I get her home, and I think she can tell that I'm annoyed with her about the grocery store and the extra time we had to spend at the customer service. I'm in a hurry today. She looks at me with her usual stare, knowing I'm in a rush to be done.

I speak to Valerie that night and tell her about my dream of forgetting to pick up Clara, and how Clara smacked me. I'm curious if this is my own manifestation of the frustration I am feeling. I wonder if Valerie feels any of the same emotions I do. I also wonder about Joy, and

111

how she feels. At some point, I plan to ask them. It seems I'm accumulating so many mental notes and I'm not sure how many I will be able to remember.

Sunday, September 4, 2011

I am at Rainbow Foods today with Ted and the girls. The butcher who is usually working when I am there shopping with Clara is behind the meat counter. He sees me and makes a comment about me being on my own today, without Clara. He asks if I am related to, or live with, Clara. I explain the situation—that I am a volunteer.

"She's kind of a pain in the butt," he says with a little smile.

Tuesday, September 6, 2011

Clara calls me and says she has some bad news. She had fallen at night and hit her face and head. "My eyes are as swollen as the bunion on Shirley's foot." *What kind of person makes a comment like that? And who is Shirley?* I let it go.

She isn't sure if she will shop tomorrow. However, she asks if I can still come over, because she can't get the door down on her new washer. She also says, "The little, short, fat women who came to clean last week made the curtain come out of the rings in the shower." She wants me to fix that, and also pick up some things at the store before I come over.

I am worried about her fall and ask if she needs to go to the doctor. She tells me no. I ask her several questions to make sure she is coherent. I email the JFCS to tell them about her fall and that she doesn't want to see a doctor. I tell them I will see her tomorrow and make sure she is okay.

items exactly as she wants. She is so picky. I start with the grapes. It takes me a while until I get the exact amount for the free pound. Seriously, grape by grape, I weigh them to get exactly one pound. There is a nice woman there who is trying to help me get the right amount. I am anxious—and annoyed at myself for feeling this way.

The woman is getting irritated by my grape problem, too. She does not like that I am taking one grape out of the bag and putting it back with the other grapes. She puts the grapes I pull out of my bag back into another bag. The woman finally offers to give me her already-weighed grapes. She may be as nuts as I am.

I spend a lot of time at the tomatoes. I want to make sure I get tomatoes that Clara will be happy with. I next try to find the shortest, fattest romaine lettuce I can find. I get jumbo eggs and ten cans of vegetables. After I check out at the register, I make sure Clara's receipt is correct. I don't want to have any problems and have to go to the customer service line, as it seems we always do when I'm shopping with Clara.

Before I go up to her apartment, I look for the bank receipt in my wallet. I can't find it. I can't believe I've lost it! I am desperate. I know the receipt has to be here. I made sure to put it in a safe place, knowing Clara would need it. It's as if someone is playing a joke on me. Once I calm myself down, I look for it again and find it. I get her groceries up to her apartment, and Clara writes me a check for $16.93, the total of her items. She is sitting at her dining room table paying her bills, and she apologizes for being such a problem. I assure her that she is not a problem.

Once I get home, I talk with the social worker at the JFCS to let them know Clara is fine after her fall. I seem to spend more time on Clara's things than I do on my own.

Friday, September 9, 2011

It's Friday, and I call Clara to see how she is. She says okay, but she can't start her washer. I just showed her how to use it the week before. I obviously didn't show her very well, though. I decide to stop by her apartment. She is in the same blue robe she was in the last time I saw her. Her eyes are more purple, but less swollen, and she looks a little better. I have her set the washer herself so she will know how to do it after I leave.

She goes to her chair to sit and mentions that her TV still turns on in the middle of the night. She also says that she's thinking about getting a new TV. After the story she told me about the washer/dryer purchase, there's no way I'm going to take her to look for a TV. I tell her that I can look at her TV again if she wants, but that if she does want to purchase a new TV, maybe Joy should take her. Clara stares at me and says, "Let it go." This curmudgeon of an old woman who will bicker over a coupon to save a few cents and who seems to have almost no patience for anything, again says, "Let it go."

These three words have become a theme for the two of us. She says them at just the time I think I can't take it anymore. The words, in fact, calm me.

Saturday, September 10, 2011

My daughters and I are working at the high school Nordic team garage sale fund-raiser today. It's one of those large neighborhood sales that remind me of the state fair, with all the people going up and down the streets. I can't get the car anywhere near the home where we're supposed to be, so I drop the girls off a few blocks away and go park down the road. I walk back. Earlier this week, I delivered and donated several bags of clothes to the sale, including Clara's forgotten bag of clothes that had been in my garage all summer.

When I arrive at the house where I'm supposed to help out, I talk with another parent about the fact that we both grew up in the same neighborhood. We somehow get on the subject of the items that were donated for the sale. Apparently, she was one of the sorters and helped set up the sale. She proceeds to tell me about a bag of old slips and stained underwear that she couldn't believe had been donated—that they tossed. I must have turned a shade of red. *Do I say something, or just pretend that it wasn't me?*

As is my nature, I have to tell, and I confess the entire story. We have a good laugh about it, my laugh more embarrassing than hers. I still don't know why I bothered to keep Clara's bag of old clothes for so long—or at all. Maybe I saw some use in them for someone. Other people clearly thought not. I'm glad they were tossed. Who wants someone else's old stained underwear?

Wednesday, September 14, 2011

Clara still doesn't want to go out. She says she can't see well, and that she can't use her glasses yet, either. Her face is still a bit swollen. Clara doesn't know how to clean the lint out of her dryer. I show her how to do it, not sure if she will be able to remember after I leave. The dryer door is so tight; she can hardly open and close it. We review the starter on the washer again. She gives me a list of items to shop for.

Byerly's for Jewish rye bread
Rainbow—8 peaches, .98/lb
Rainbow—4 Golden Delicious green apples, .95/lb
Rainbow—lake trout ¾ lb fattest piece
Milk, Kemps Select 1% ½ gallon

I first go to Byerly's to get her the Jewish rye bread. My next stop is at Rainbow for peaches and Golden Delicious apples. The store has both large and small apples today, so I call Clara to ask her which she prefers. I have to shout into the phone for her to hear me.

I pick out lake trout, which the butcher helps me with—the fattest one, of course. The butcher cuts a half-pound piece. Again, I call Clara to make sure this is okay with her. The butcher knows Clara, and understands my worries.

Next, I get the milk. Checkout. Done! I think I finish in record time.

Wait, I better check my receipt. I see that I've been charged incorrectly for the apples! I go over and stand in line at the customer service desk. The clerk gives me the difference back in cash. I explain that I am shopping for an elderly woman. The clerk knows right away who I am referring to. The clerk senses my anxiety, and takes extra time to go through the receipt with me to make sure everything else is correct. Even though I have to spend time at the customer service counter, it is still easier to shop without Clara. As I walk out of the store, a pang of guilt sticks in my stomach because of this thought.

It's interesting how my life has turned into a shopping list. I think I'm dreaming about lists, seeing them any time I close my eyes.

When I get back to Clara's with her groceries, she sees the peaches and thinks they're the apples. She makes the mistake of thinking that the apples I brought home (which are really peaches) are red and not green. I can see that irritated look on her face. She is angry until she realizes the red color is of the peaches. Knowing the story of Valerie bringing home a nectarine instead of a peach by

accident, I know what can happen in a situation like this. This time I was able to avoid a disaster somehow.

As I put away her groceries, I mention that I am going to Cub Foods when I leave. Clara politely asks if I will get her a few things, too. She hands me a coupon. Why can't I just say no to her? Or why did I even mention I was going to Cub?

I go to Cub Foods, and then return to Clara's with her groceries. As I put the second round of groceries away, Clara says, "The ice cream is on sale at Walgreens." She stares at me with the Clara look, hoping that I will go to Walgreens for the ice cream. I don't have the time; the ice cream will have to wait.

Clara gives me a check for her groceries.

As I'm about to leave, I ask Clara if she wants to go out to lunch again. She responds, "No, you don't eat enough." She must be referring to our lunch last winter.

As I often do, I go over our conversations in my head as I get in my car and drive away. Clara seems to have more than enough money to live on. I don't know much about her finances; however, she doesn't seem to be struggling. I don't know why she won't buy ice cream for herself when she wants it. She refuses to buy it unless it's on sale. I wonder who's going to go through all of her stuff after she dies. Will any of her relatives want her things? More importantly, will anyone even acknowledge her passing?

I'm curious to know what Clara was like when she was younger. It would be interesting to talk to some of her relatives who knew her as a child or even a teen. I'm not sure if I will get the chance to talk to anyone, though.

Wednesday, September 21, 2011

Last night I had another awful nightmare about Clara. This time I went to visit, or pick her up, and she was acting insane from being cooped up in her apartment for so long. She was throwing things, clawing at me, and screaming. During part of the dream, she was also lying on her bed seeming a bit out of it, like she was in a daze.

I wonder what it means. Is it a premonition? Or is it just my emotions affecting me?

Today Clara has a list of things to do. Most important, though, is getting the six boxes of Total cereal on sale with a coupon. When we get to the grocery store, she buys fresh green beans, something different from the items on her regular list! As usual, one of her items rings up incorrectly at the register and we have to get it corrected at the customer service counter.

After the grocery store, we head over to the clinic where Clara has her blood drawn to pick up her prescription at the pharmacy there. In the car, she tells me about a phone conversation she had with the pharmacist regarding price and the amount of pills. She expresses that she isn't confident they are going to get it right. After what happened at the Walgreens pharmacy, there is no way I'm going inside this pharmacy with her. I drop her off at the door and cross my fingers as I watch her walk in on her own.

She's in there a long time, and I start to get nervous. When she finally comes out, she tells me they didn't have her prescription filled when she got there, so she had to wait. I'm glad she waited and didn't come to the car all angry. After the pharmacy, she wants to go to Sally Beauty Supply to get a hair trimmer for her facial hair. Her beard is the worst I've seen on a woman. She pulls on the hairs all the time.

Sally doesn't have electric trimmers, so we go to Target, where they have a large selection, but she can't decide on one. She wants one with a cord that she can plug in. Most of the trimmers are battery operated with a charger. We leave without one, which is too bad. It's hard to look at her with all that white stringy hair on her chin. On our way out, I see my friend Judy. We briefly talk about me volunteering with Clara. Judy tells me that she's also out doing shopping for an elderly couple.

During our drive to Rainbow, we talk about the cost of school lunch. Clara remembers that I had told her I make my children's lunches each day. She tells me again that, as a child, she lived half a block from school, and would go home every day for lunch. Her mom would make a very large lunch: meat and potatoes. I ask her if she has any photos. She tells me that she has none from when she was a child.

I ask Clara if she needs help sorting through her things. She tells me that her closets are packed full with stuff. I really want to ask her who is responsible for going through her things after she's gone. However, I don't ask. It seems as though Clara doesn't think about her mortality. That's probably why she's lived so long. She never says, "When I am gone," or "After I'm gone . . ."

Cub Foods is our next stop. I see my friend Judy again. We laugh about the fact that we're doing the same things today. It is the usual shopping with Clara. She buys a lot of meat and fish. We go through the checkout lane and she checks her receipt. She realizes she has bought a pack of chicken legs and not thighs. Now how did that get by me? I know that Clara only eats chicken thighs and not legs. I'm usually so careful about making sure she buys exactly what she is shopping for. I hate wasting time standing at the customer service counter to correct things. We have to return the legs and get the thighs. It seems like there's always something.

Clara has her pacemaker appointment coming up. She tells me they don't have any appointments for Wednesday, our usual shopping day. She made the appointment for Monday and asks if I could take her then. I tell her that I have to check my schedule. I can't say yes to everything. I have a life, too, although sometimes it doesn't seem that way. I don't want to set a precedent where I'm giving in to her consistently increasing requests.

After I get home and check my schedule, I call her and tell her I won't be able to take her on Monday. I suggest she call Joy or a company that helps transport seniors to appointments.

Wednesday, September 28, 2011

I pick up Clara. She smells terrible: a combination of stale food and something rancid, like she did not wipe properly after she used the bathroom. She looks a little tired.

I take her to her blood-work appointment at the clinic. I drop her off and then go over to the AAA to look for a new purse—the one I use every day is almost falling apart—and a map of Michigan for when Margie and I visit a college there. I find a purse that I like but I don't buy it because I want to check around to see if any other stores are selling it for a lower price.

When I get back to the clinic, Clara isn't ready yet, so I go and fill up my car with gas. When she does finally come out, she says it was crowded and she almost left. I'm glad that she didn't, because I would have had to bring her back again. We then go to Rainbow. She wants a package of single-roll toilet paper. It's about time. We have been shopping together since January and she has yet to buy toilet paper. I find her a four pack of cheap toilet paper for $.99. She thinks about it for a while, and finally says she is using Kleenex because she doesn't have toilet paper. *What?* I make her take the toilet paper. She gets eight cans of pears and peaches, but she needs ten for the discount, which we don't realize until we get to the register to check out, so I have to run back and get two more cans.

Back at her apartment, I do the usual: help her get the lint out of the dryer. She scrapes the lint out with her long nails. It drives me nuts. It's like fingernails on a chalkboard.

Clara pulls out some photos to look at and starts opening up a little about her background. Clara tells me that she was born in Duluth. Her parents moved to Superior because it was too hard to pull the cart up the hill in Duluth. Superior is more flat. They then moved to Cooley, Minnesota, where her father had the grocery store that burned down. The Nashwauk Fire Department came but the hoses didn't work in the fire hydrant in Cooley. Clara told me they just had to watch the grocery store burn. She lived in the building, upstairs from the store.

Thursday, October 6, 2011

Clara called me Tuesday night and asked if we could shop on Thursday or Friday instead of Wednesday because the management company was sending someone to fix her door that has been broken since the fire in June. Clara had been calling them, but they had not done anything about it. I finally called them myself to see if I could get things moving along. Seems my call might have worked!

I pick her up at 9:00 a.m. I know we're going grocery shopping and then to Sears to get a trimmer for her facial hair. To save time and not have to go back to her apartment, I bring a cooler and ice so we can put her cold items in there while we drive between stores.

We shop at Cub Foods first. It is the usual round and round the store using coupons. She has to spend at least $50.00 to use the $5.00-off coupon. I worry about this as we shop. After Clara finishes shopping, she asks me to add up the prices to see if she is at $50.00 yet. How can I add up this stuff without knowing the prices? I try as best I can. But Clara is not sure that my total is correct, so we go back to the fruits and vegetables and then to the meats for more packages of chicken and fish.

I pay for my groceries in the self-checkout lane. I am trying to get through the morning quickly because I have to get to my kids' school conferences. Luckily, when Clara gets to the register her groceries are over $50.00, and she gets to use the $5.00-off coupon. I am anxious thinking about what we would have done if they weren't. I tell her to check her receipt. It is all fine. But she still hems and haws over it as if it is wrong. I just can't understand this. We get to the car and put her groceries that need to be refrigerated in the cooler.

I pull up to the lower level of Sears, hoping she won't have to go upstairs. I'm not sure which department the trimmers are in, but Clara insists they are in housewares. I drop her at the machinery and tools door, then park the car before meeting her inside. She is looking for a chair to sit down in, but no chairs are available. I track down a cart she can hold on to. She barely makes it twenty feet before she wants to sit.

I find her a spot on a display bed to sit, and track down a salesperson to help us find an electric hair trimmer. We leave Clara sitting on the bed. The salesperson takes me to the electric trimmers and I try to figure out which one will be the best. Clara makes her way over to us and agrees to purchase the $43.00 electric razor/trimmer plug in.

On our way to the register, Clara has chest pain and wants to stop to rest. I am worried for her. We stop for a moment and then continue on. She hands the clerk an expired Sears card. Here we go again, another fifteen minutes added to our shopping. Clara says it is impossible that the card is expired, because they just sent her the card. I look at the card and tell her it's expired and that she probably threw out the new one and kept the old one by mistake. The clerk asks her to put her Social Security number into the machine where customers swipe their credit cards. Clara doesn't want to give her number.

I don't blame her, because I don't like to give out my Social Security number, either. However, I explain to Clara that the only way she can use her Sears card is to give her Social Security Number so they can look her up. She agrees and punches it in. She must have done it too slowly, because it's not working. I have to reenter the number for her. She then has to show her Minnesota identification card. Finally, we finish, and unexpectedly, the bill is less than the quoted price, so it isn't all bad. Clara leaves with a satisfied smile.

We arrive back at her apartment, and I am worried about the razor and want to make sure it will be the right one for her. With the TV remote issues and other things, I'm guarded like this now. I put together the razor and show her how it works.

I explain that she needs to use the trimmer first before using the razor, because her hair is too long. This is what the salesperson had suggested. I have her hold the razor, turn it on and off, and then open and close the trimmer. She insists that I should be the one to put the razor to her chin and begin trimming her beard. I do so reluctantly. I am able to trim away the long, twisted, white hairs before switching to the razor to shave the area clean of hair.

I can feel the choking of vomit in my throat. She wants me to trim and shave more, but I just can't. I am nauseated and grossed out. I finally have to tell her that I need to get to my kids' conferences and she will need to finish on her own. The white wiry hair is everywhere, even on her couch where we are sitting.

This is not what I signed up for when I agreed to be a volunteer. I am very uncomfortable. She mentions that her old razor had broken a while back. I wonder if Valerie was helping her shave before me. I sometimes feel like I am being taken advantage of because of everything I do for her. I have a hard time saying no to Clara. She seems to be grateful, though, which makes me feel good, but at the same time I feel bad for thinking that she is taking advantage of me.

As I leave, I ask her if she has any friends that she still keeps in touch with. She gives me a blank stare. I ask her about friends when she was younger. It seems as though she really doesn't have many. I can feel the tears in my eyes welling up, but I hold them back.

Wednesday, October 12, 2011

Clara needs to go back to the clinic because the doctor sent in the wrong order with her last blood work. They mistakenly tested her cholesterol, not her thyroid. Last time Clara was at the clinic, I stopped in at the AAA to check out the purses and found one that I liked. I have been searching around to see if any other stores have it for a cheaper price. AAA has the best price. While Clara is at her appointment, I go back to AAA and purchase the purse. Good or bad, Clara must be rubbing off on me. I find myself constantly checking my receipts and shopping for lower prices.

After the clinic, we go to the bank. I drop her off. She says it might take a while because she has a bunch of change in her purse that she's going to cash into dollars. She says her purse is getting too heavy. Sure enough, it takes a while. After she comes out, I ask where she wants to shop. She says she still has enough food left from last week, so doesn't need anything today. I am completely surprised! This is the first time in almost a year she doesn't want to go to some grocery store. I'm hoping this is a sign for the better.

We go back to her apartment and we clean out her dryer lint trap, as we do each week now. It's the same routine. I get the lint trap and she scrapes out the lint with her fingernails.

I sit down to talk with her. Clara tells me more family stories. She also tells me that all of her stories are personal and private, and I am not allowed to repeat them. Of course, I will respect her wishes.

Wednesday, October 19, 2011

I call Clara before I leave home to pick her up for our weekly shopping, but there is no answer. I'm always a bit concerned when there is no answer. However, I know she can't always hear the phone because her TV is too loud.

I call her again when I arrive at her apartment, and she answers. She wants to go to Rainbow because they have the things she needs today. However, she also wants to go to Cub because they have good prices on tomatoes and yams. I suggest that we go to Cub first to get the tomatoes and yams. In a stern voice Clara says, "No, I want to go to Rainbow first and see what their prices are." *Ugh!*

In the car, we talk about investing money. She tells me she has too much in her checking account, and talks of purchasing a municipal bond. I tell her about a bond I found recently that goes out to 2031. She thinks that would be good for her, too. Would she actually consider this? I'm thinking about the fact that the bond goes out twenty years, and that Clara would be 112 years old.

She doesn't seem to consider her mortality. What a great way to live! I tell her she shouldn't keep a lot of money in her checking account. She laughs about my comment and responds, "No one can get a hold of my checking account, because the checkbook is always with me, either at home or in my purse." It's one of the first times Clara alludes to having any kind of money. I know she has enough to live on, but with how frugal she is, I assume that it's not much. I wonder how much she thinks a lot is: $1,000, or maybe $5,000? Who knows?

Off to Rainbow Foods we go. It's the usual romaine lettuce, carrots, rye bread, and bananas today. After we pass through the fruits and vegetables, I ask to see her list. She wants broccoli. I suggest we go back to the vegetables and get it. She says we will do it after we go down the aisles for the other items. I still can't understand why she has to go back to the fruits and vegetables after we've already been there. It wastes time and drives me crazy.

She has a coupon for chunk cheese, and I have no idea what chunk cheese is. I have to find a store employee just to find out that it is the same thing as block cheese. We get the cheese and orange juice, which she has a coupon for, too. We check out the ice cream. It's $6.99. Clara shakes her head; too much money. We next get four boxes of Total cereal. All the boxes are stuck together. I try as hard as I can to pull them apart. I can't, and have to get a customer service person to help. Clara, of course, has a coupon for the Total and it is on sale.

We still have time for a visit to Cub Foods, and Clara surprises me with another one of those coupons for $5.00

off when you spend $50.00. At Cub, she wants me to add the groceries in her cart. She should know by now that I can't add! I never get anything right that she asks me to add, and she always bluntly points out my errors. Things are no different this time. To add to the trouble, we have to roam around looking for things to make $50.00. We choose a few cans of red salmon and canned fruit to make sure we meet the limit.

The stress is too much for me, especially when I am getting tired and irritated. Lately it seems I'm having a harder time dealing with her smell. Luckily, when we check out, her bill is $55.00. No problems with the coupon.

I get her home, and we clean the dryer lint trap. She gives me coupons for the gas station.

Before I leave, I notice some new plants in her living room near the sliding door to the deck. I tell her they're very nice. She says Valerie brought them to her. What a nice thing to do. I still wonder about their relationship.

After I leave, I decide I better use the coupon Clara gave me and go to the gas station near my house. I have to go in to the station and ask how to use the coupon. They tell me to push the "pay inside" button on the pump. I fill my gas tank and it's $47.94. I go back inside with the coupon; the gas costs me $47.01. I save $.93. With the extra time I took to go inside twice, I'm not sure the $.93 is worth it. I feel guilty thinking this way, and for not wanting to use the coupon.

Wednesday, October 26, 2011

I pick up Clara today. The weather is getting colder, but it's almost November, so that's expected. She has on her usual blue coat, white stockings, and blue slip-on shoes. They're the same unsteady ones she always wears. They look like old lady flip-flops. Her socks are saggy and her toes hang off the front. She has her usual beat-up dark-blue purse and she hands it to me when she gets in my car. The same stale smell follows her. I'm still not sure where the smell comes from.

She wants to go to both Rainbow and Cub today. Why can't she just get everything she needs at one grocery store? I remind myself that I usually need to go to several grocery stores to get what I need, too. As we drive to Rainbow, she asks me how the college search for my older daughter is going. I tell Clara that my daughter's first choice at this point is a college out west. She wants to know why I would send her away and spend that kind of money, when she can stay at home for free and attend the University of Minnesota. I explain that my daughter needs to go off to college and live away from home—and that

142

her sisters have been waiting fifteen years to get her out of
the house. Clara laughs at my comment. I also tell Clara
that even if my daughter were to go to school locally, she
wouldn't live at home. I tell Clara that the U of M is just
too big for my daughter.

Clara can't understand any of this. She seems disgusted
at the thought of spending so much money unnecessarily.
Sometimes I feel we would really have a battle if I push
a disagreement, even one that has to do with my life and
my family. I have to let things go with her. We also get
on the subject of Social Security checks and pensions.
Clara tells me that the amount on her Social Security
check goes down each year. She was receiving $700.00
for a while and now gets around $650.00. She mentions
that she could never live on $700.00 alone. Luckily, she
also gets her pension from her previous job. Between the
two checks, she has enough.

We discuss the fact that she has been retired for almost
thirty years. She likes to correct me. I say "thirty" and she
says "close to thirty." Clara retired at exactly sixty-five
and a half. I guess it doesn't surprise me that she's so exact
about this. She thinks the Social Security office wishes she
would die already. I tell her that she is probably going to
live a lot longer. She says that some days she doesn't feel
like that at all. I am surprised she says this. This is the first
time I've ever heard her speak of her mortality. I feel sad
for her.

She also tells me about the fact that she has so much to
do—things like call the JFCS and figure out what day her
housekeeper is coming—but can't get anything done. She

also can't find the cleaning bill she left on the table. Given how messy it is, I can understand why. I encourage her to make the call. Hopefully, she'll take care of it.

At times I think about how different Clara and I are. She is good at numbers, and has no qualms speaking her mind, even if it upsets people. Me, I'm more sensitive and don't like to hurt people's feelings. I'm also terrible with numbers. Yet we share many similarities, too, like being crabby; yes, I can be crabby, too. In fact, when I was young, my family used to call me "Mrs. Crabtree." And then there's the fact that Clara and I both overthink things and struggle with the inability to let things go.

There is also a quirkiness about Clara that I can relate to. My children see a quirkiness in me and describe me as being a bit weird—not weird in a bad way, but just odd in my thinking and antics. That's how I think of Clara. Clara and I are also both a bit obsessive, she with shopping, newspapers, and coupons, and me with a whole slew of things. When I'm not working, taking care of my family, or volunteering, I'm researching various topics: animals, diseases, plants, foods, and history. My favorite research topic is maps, though. I love formulating and creating directional routes to various locations. Maybe it's my unusual brain's way of trying to stay organized. I have also noticed that Clara and I are both stubborn and independent. The alikeness that I find most interesting— one that is related to this trait—is our need to be alone more often than not. Not alone together, but away from people altogether. I'm not speaking for Clara, and she's never described herself this way to me; it's just an observation. But given how she acts, I wonder if she spent a lot of time alone when she was younger. I am starting to see myself in her. Am I going to be like her when I'm ninety-three?

When we get to Rainbow Foods, I drop her at the door as I usually do. I get in and out of the car to help her each time I drop her off and pick her up. The first few weeks, I would forget to buckle and unbuckle her as I helped her in and out of the car. She would always have to remind me. Now it's so automatic that I hardly think about it.

At Rainbow, Clara gets fish, cottage cheese, bananas, tomatoes, and barley. I ask her what she is planning to make with the barley. She says soup. I decide to get barley, too. As we check out together, Clara looks over my groceries, scrutinizing them. We leave Rainbow and drive to Cub. In the car, Clara asks me if my husband agrees with my daughter's college choices. I tell her yes, and leave it at that. I don't want to take the college discussion any further with her today.

I drop Clara at the door. When I get inside, she's in her scooter and not moving. She's pushing the button and wondering why it won't move. It's the same thing each week when the scooter is plugged in. I tell her every time that the cart needs to be unplugged to work. She can never remember this. *She is so bright; how can she not remember?*

I unplug the scooter and she is still pushing the button, not understanding why it won't go now that it is unplugged. I see that it is turned off. I push the "on" button and off she goes.

Clara looks at all the squash, and I watch her try to lift them. She can barely lift things now, especially from her angle in her scooter. I have to lift the squash for her. I ask if she cooks them before she cuts them, imagining that she must struggle to make them for herself. She says there is no way she can possibly cut through an uncooked squash.

It is the usual routine with the fish. She looks at the salmon and sees it came from Chile and she shakes her head, as if disappointed. Clara moves on to meats. I'm not sure if she is going to buy more after all the meat she bought both last week and two weeks ago. Nevertheless, I run to get some bags, because I know what I can expect if she begins to sort through the meat.

By the time I get back, she has all the packages of steak on her purse in her lap. I'm so grossed out. *How can she not care about the raw meat and germs? I just don't get it.* She turns the packages every which way, inspecting each from every angle and side, and finally shakes them. She does this with every package of meat and chicken, and once she finishes, she starts all over again with the same packages.

She eventually picks two packages of kosher steaks. I ask if she's eaten the meat from last week. She says that she's had some. I also ask if she froze any. She says yes. However, I'm not so sure, because often when I unload her groceries, I see the previous week's packages still in the refrigerator. Why should this week be any different? I start to get anxious about the packages of meat being contaminated. My mind spins ahead; I wonder if I have antibacterial cleaner in the car or not, knowing that I can't wash my hands at her place because there is no soap and nowhere to dry them and if I try to use a tissue or paper towel, Clara will get upset.

I make her get more toilet paper. Four rolls for $1.00. She tells me that Rainbow's price is $.99 for four rolls, and I nearly fall over, surprised Clara doesn't want to drive back to Rainbow to save a penny.

I have our system for checking out and bagging the groceries down now. I stuff the bags as much as I can, because it's easier for me to carry fewer bags up to her apartment. She has way too many bags in her apartment, anyway. I always ask her what she's going to do with all her paper bags. Clara tells me her cousin Joy likes to have them. So far, I haven't seen any of the bags leave her place—even after she's seen Joy.

As we drive home, she asks again, what Ted thinks of Margie's going away to college. The answer still hasn't changed.

When we get back to her apartment, I realize her building is beginning to smell normal, which is nice, since I am getting tired of the burnt smell from the summer fire. I carry the two heavy grocery bags up to her apartment, unpack them, and proceed to the lint trap. She continues to toss the lint in the toilet; she's been doing this routinely, even though I have told her in the past it will clog the plumbing. But she just laughs, and says her bowel movement will clog it more than the lint will.

As I pass by her bedroom, I glance in and can see she has two mattress pads: one that she sleeps on and one that she uses to cover herself. She has no sheet and no blankets—nothing—but I don't say anything to her. Instead, I mention that she should toss away or recycle all the bags in her kitchen that are taking up room. Her kitchen makes her look like a hoarder. Clara asks me to take bags filled with recycling down to the recycling in the garage. I ask her to go with me. She refuses, but tells me to go get the red grocery cart in the basement and bring it up to load the bags into it so it's easier to bring downstairs. I don't want to, but I don't say no.

In the basement, I find the cart to carry everything in. I go back up the elevator and load the cart up with six paper bags filled with recycling. I start getting anxious, knowing I will have to touch the bin with no way to wash my hands. This is difficult for me. Some days I just want to quit and say I'm done with this, that I can't handle it. Today is one of those days.

I have a hard time getting the loaded grocery cart back to the basement by myself. I feel some resentment. I want Clara to come and help me, but I guess I'm being a little unfair, considering her frailty. She'd never be able to do it. I arrive in the basement. The bins are a bit high for me to reach over and I have a hard time opening, and tossing each of the six bags in. When I am done, I leave the cart and head back up to say good-bye. My hands feel grimy. I ask Clara how she usually gets the recycling to the garage. She says her housekeeper does it.

When I arrive home, I spray my car with Lysol.

Wednesday, November 2, 2011

The first thing Clara says to me today is "I have a problem." I always get nervous when she says she has a problem. But I guess I shouldn't; her problems are really not that bad. They just tend to be time consuming. I ask what the problem is.

She says the door to the closet that houses her washer and dryer won't close. She thinks the housekeeper has caused the problem. I explain to her that sometimes if there is an uneven load in the washer, the machine will jump around and move; maybe it had moved and is blocking the door. I tell her I can probably fix the problem. But if not, I will have my husband come and take care of it. She says she doesn't think I can move the washer. I think I can. She also says she can have the maintenance person from the building move it. I ask if this person lives in her building. She says no. This causes her to go into her usual gripes about the building. I tell her I'll see what I can do about the washer once we return from shopping.

She wants to go to both Rainbow and Cub today. I tell her that before I can decide if we have time for both, I'll need to see how long it takes us at the first store. She wants ice cream at Cub Foods, so we decide to go to Rainbow first. When we get there, they don't have any available scooters. I know she can't walk, so we decide I will push her in the wheelchair with a basket attached.

It makes me self-conscious to do this. However, I instantly realize I have a lot of control over our grocery shopping when I'm responsible for her getting around. I can go as quickly as I want—and I go quickly. I can tell she's frustrated that she isn't able to do what she wants, but there's no way I'm pushing her round and round, as she likes to go in her scooter. I am going to do this efficiently and the way it should be done. We won't be going back to the spots we've already visited.

Fruits and vegetables: $.48 for a small bag of carrots, three bananas selected very carefully. Two-dollar white bread on sale and doubled bagged. A large, fat piece of cod.

I move quickly. Clara is concerned she is too heavy to push. No way. I am happy to push her fast. Next stop: the Total cereal. This must be why we're at Rainbow today. Six boxes on sale, plus she has a coupon. Somehow, we get all her groceries in the small basket attached to the wheelchair. It's amazing that all her groceries come to only $10.00, plus she gets a coupon for free milk. After sale price and coupon, the six boxes of Total were almost free. We've also saved time.

We have our usual discussions in the car. Clara is happy, which means we will stumble through our regular conversation about college as we drive to Cub Foods. I tell her that we're going to visit a school in Michigan this week. She just doesn't understand. I also tell her I won't be able to shop with her on the Wednesday before Thanksgiving. She doesn't say anything, and I wonder if she is doing anything for the holiday.

She brings up the fact that Valerie was supposed to visit her the previous weekend, but never did. Without saying it, I think Clara is deciding she'll call Valerie about going with her on the shopping day that I have to skip. I don't worry too much about the possibility that Valerie won't be able to go, either. Clara has so much food; she can skip a day, if need be.

I struggle with whether or not to ask Clara to Thanksgiving dinner at my home. Having her there will just give me added stress and responsibility. However, I feel terrible that she may be alone. Also, I'm not sure if anyone could stand to look at the hair on her face while they're eating. I know this sounds terrible, but it really isn't pleasant to look at. I feel so guilty. I'm not sure what I'll do.

We arrive at Cub Foods. Every time I drive Clara to the front door of the grocery store, she does this thing where she harshly tells me to "STOP!" She does it again today—like I don't know where to stop! I always end up blocking people walking in the crosswalk. She insists that I drop her directly at the door. I would really like to stop a couple feet to the right or left of the door, but I do it her way. She gets out of the car in a huff. I park and go into the store as usual.

She selects four cartons of Breyers ice cream. She wants to take advantage of today's deal: buy four at the sale price of $3.99 and get $4.00 back. There is another deal today, too: buy two jars of jam and get $1.00 back. Also, she has a chance to save on canned vegetables; buy six and get $2.00 back. At the register, she only gets a total of $6.00 back. I quickly try to figure out the exchange in my head. I can feel my fingers twitching as if I were back in school, trying to figure out a math problem.

They short her by $1.00. She is supposed to get $7.00 back in coupons good for future visits. Apparently, the jam didn't ring up for the $1.00 back. Of course this has to happen! The cashier is kind enough to give Clara $1.00 in cash rather than re-ringing everything to generate the coupon. If it had gone the other way, we would have to be here an extra twenty minutes. I laugh to myself; it's funny that I'm matched with a person so focused on math, and I'm terrible at it.

During the drive back to Clara's, I think about whether or not I'll be able to move the washer and dryer unit. I quickly unload the groceries and go to check out the closet door. Clara's washer and dryer unit sits on a hard plastic square pan to protect the floor. The pan is pushed out and is in the line of the door. I adjust it by moving the washer-dryer around. I also move around the cleaning supplies that are in her closet. I can see how Clara had thought the housekeeper caused the problem. However, I think the washer must have jumped during a load. After several attempts, I am able to adjust it back in place perfectly.

I have nowhere to wash my hands. They are disgusting after coming into contact with so many germs. I am stressed because I had to touch her cleaning supplies and dirty bucket. I see her bathroom. There's no way I'm washing my hands here—again, I'm grossed out!

Wednesday, November 9, 2011

I look for my camera today so I can take some pictures
of Clara. I really want to have a good one of her. We've
spent so much time together. I get scared thinking that
one of these Wednesdays I will find her dead. I feel guilty
when I think this. Sometimes I feel that I've gotten myself
into something I can't handle. *Will today be the day?* I
feel sad thinking that our time together will eventually
end. However, other times I feel overwhelmed and look
forward to not having the stress and responsibility of
helping her any more.

I'm not sure why I keep volunteering to help Clara
each week. But I would never think of leaving her. She
depends on me, and I depend on her in some strange
way. Maybe it's because I feel that she needs me. I grew
up with a lot of stress and chaos, so maybe the more stress
and chaos I have in my life, the more normal things feel. I
have become an expert at managing a life like that. I think
my siblings needed me to keep the family from arguing
when we were all young; they never said that, exactly,
but I could sense they needed me to intervene and try

to make things okay, even though I couldn't always do it. Maybe I still want to feel that I'm needed that way. Maybe I do the same thing with Clara. I don't know, but it is who I am. I'm committed to her.

I call Clara on my way to pick her up and she doesn't answer. When I get to her building, I use the lobby phone to call her. Clara answers in her usual low "Hallow?" I tell her that I'm here. She says, "You're here? I'll be right down." She comes out the door dressed completely in blue. She has on her blue strap shoes, blue socks, blue pants, blue shirt, and blue coat—all different shades of blue. I help her out to the car. She doesn't smell. I know it will be a good day.

I know she needs to go to the bank because she hasn't gone for a while, so I ask, and she says she does. On our way to Byerly's, she asks me about the Michigan trip. I tell her that Margie enjoyed visiting the school, but doesn't feel that it's the one for her. I also tell Clara about Margie liking Duluth when we drove through the city at night. We again have our weekly conversation about the cost of college. Clara's tuition for her senior year in college was $5,000.00, and she paid $20.00 a month for a room in a house with other girls. I laugh to myself, realizing how much has changed since Clara attended college at the University of Minnesota.

I drop Clara off at the door to the store. She will visit the bank first, and she tells me to come in after I park and check with the meat department about getting kosher turkey legs and thighs for Thanksgiving. Once I park the car, I make my way to the kosher meat department and speak with the butcher. He says he will be able to cut up a turkey for Clara. After Clara is done at the bank, I get her a cart to hold on to and we walk over to the butcher. Clara settles on two turkey thighs and legs, the smallest weight possible; she'll come back for them next Wednesday.

We get in the car and I ask her where she wants to shop. She wants to go to Rainbow and then Cub Foods. As usual, I tell her we'll have to see how much time is left after Rainbow; that will determine if we have time to go to the other store. I have to be home by twelve thirty. She gives me another one of her usual responses: "Oh, all right."

Shopping at Cub Foods today is a bit unorganized. When we pull into the parking lot, I see a large tent with cars everywhere. They are hosting the Salvation Army's Red Kettle Kickoff. I'm curious to see if Clara will put anything in the red kettle. She doesn't: not a thing—as I suspected. I add two coins on my way in. Clara heads directly to the meat first. She has her $5.00-off coupon if she spends $50.00. After analyzing all the available kosher steaks, she selects three for $10.00 each. *We are at $30.00.* I repeat the total over and over in my head.

I ask if I can take a few pictures of her, and she wants to know why. I tell her that they're for my scrapbook, and that I want memories of us shopping. She says, "I can give you a picture." I tell her that would be a picture of when I didn't know her. I want a photo of her during the time we shopped together. I take a picture of her when she has three packages of meat on her lap.

I decide I better get my own cart and do some grocery shopping. I run around trying to find the same $5.00-off coupon that Clara has. However, I don't see one in any circulars. When I catch up with Clara, I see she has six large cans of tomatoes. The cans are on sale with a coupon, of course. She then tells me that she is frustrated. I think she gets a bit stressed when she has to figure how to spend $50.00 to get $5.00 off. She adds a few more items to her cart and asks me to add it up. *Okay, three steaks, two sweet potatoes, one jar of salad dressing, and six cans of tomatoes.* It looks like no more than $40.00. We go back to the steaks for one more to hit the $50.00 mark. *She does not need this much food,* I think. I don't say anything to her, though.

I go through checkout with my groceries first. Clara's bill after coupons and discount is $42.00. I can't help but think that she probably won't use all the cans of tomatoes, and the steaks will likely sit in her freezer with all the other meat from weeks past. Is she really saving money? Wouldn't she spend less if she only buys what she needs?

I load the groceries in my car, and go back to pick up Clara at the door. She tells me that she only needs a few things at Rainbow. I actually don't mind the extra stop today. I try to find humor in it all. I tell Clara that if I push her around in the wheelchair, shopping will go more quickly. She laughs and thinks I'm joking. I'm not!

I ask Clara to look over her list in the car so I can get an idea for my plan to get her through Rainbow quickly.

I am determined to get out of the store quickly because I have other places I need to be today.

I drop Clara at the front door. After parking the car, I find her still on her scooter, plugged into the wall. She is sitting there wondering why the scooter won't work. It's the same problem as before. It has to be unplugged for it to work.

After I unplug her, she stops at the romaine lettuce. I sense this isn't going to be a quick shopping episode. I know what's on her grocery list and decide to keep her on task. From the lettuce, we quickly stop at the carrots. Off to the bread—Jewish rye. We speed by the meats. Not today. We run to the dairy and grab sour cream, milk, and eggs. Then we go back in a circle for two pounds of butter. Next she decides she wants to look at the ice cream. I remind her that she got four cartons last week, and ask if she has eaten any. She says she has only finished one carton, but the ice cream is on sale.

I am ready to leave and she remembers she wants grape tomatoes. I should have said something earlier, because I know she buys tomatoes each week and today she passed by them. I can't help but think that Clara tricked me into going to Rainbow by telling me she only needed a few items. As we go back to the vegetables, I realize how naive I am to think we will get out quickly. Of course, the cherry tomatoes aren't marked on sale as they should be. I always get nervous when the things Clara wants aren't marked properly, because we usually have a problem at the register. I pick a container of tomatoes and cross my fingers.

The wait is long at the register. Wednesdays are for coupon enthusiasts. It's amazing how cheaply you can eat, especially if you are not particular about what you eat.

As we drive back to her place, I ask if she did this kind of shopping when she drove. She gives me a funny look, and I explain that I meant to ask if she went to several grocery stores one after the other, or to just one store, when she shopped on her own.

"I have always had to go to different stores to get the best prices," she replies. I wonder if she ever thought about the money she spent on gas.

The parking lot of Clara's apartment complex is always full of trucks now because of the construction on the burned units in her building. The lot is small and I have a hard time maneuvering my car around the trucks. I drop Clara at the door, and then drag her heavy grocery bags into the lobby and up to her apartment. She knows I am in a hurry and tells me not to unload the groceries, but calls me over to the washer. I have to remove the lint trap from the dryer.

As I get ready to leave, I ask if I can take a picture of her in her blue-and-white-striped chair. She says she doesn't look good and would rather give me a different picture. She starts looking through a stack of old photos. I tell her that she can look after I leave and give it to me next week. She quickly finds a photo of herself that she feels is acceptable. It is of her sitting in a chair, maybe at a table. She looks heavier and several years younger.

I don't take the picture with me. It's not the Clara I shop with.

I race home and unload my groceries, spray the car with Lysol, and go to drop off a headband at my youngest daughter's school. I switch cars with Margie and make it to my 1:00 p.m. meeting.

I can't help but think that my time with Clara is happening for a reason. I'm not sure what that purpose is, though. Our shopping, as well as the time we spend together, is very strange. It always seems like these unusual situations follow me—or I follow them. I have this need to help people all the time and people seem to find me, too. I guess it was inevitable that I was going to be matched with the person who needed help the most.

Tuesday, November 15, 2011

It's Tuesday night, and as usual, I have mixed feelings about shopping with Clara tomorrow. I sometimes wish I didn't have to volunteer with her. I just don't want to do this anymore. I'm so busy with work, family, and other activities—nothing unusual, but the ordinary, everyday family and adult stuff that takes so much time and attention. The stress with Clara makes me frustrated. I have to keep reminding myself how much she needs me. And I have to remind myself that there are also times I enjoy shopping with her, and look forward to our shopping days. Each Wednesday seems like a different episode of a comedy show. Will she answer the phone? Will she still be here? Is she going to smell? How many different places are we going to have to go?

I haven't asked her to Thanksgiving yet. I feel so guilty about not asking her. I know she won't come over, but what if she does? She smells, and we'll all have to look at the hair on her face. Moreover, she'll have to use my bathroom, which will make for extra cleanup. I wonder if anyone has invited her to celebrate the holiday. I'm sure not. I wonder how she feels that no one invites her. Maybe she's used to it.

I had another dream about Clara. They are coming more frequently. I dreamt that I went to get Clara and I brought the truck. I then had to grocery shop for her because she couldn't get into the truck. Is this an indicator that we won't be able to shop together in the near future? I'm sad thinking about it. I feel so conflicted.

I sense that Clara has to force herself to be nice to me. I guess it's mutual because I sometimes feel like I have to do the same. She knows I'm a volunteer and she doesn't want to risk losing me. I wonder if I just think this, or if it is actually real. I feel it, though.

Wednesday, November 16, 2011

I call Clara before I leave my house.

"Hi, Clara; it's Beth."

"Oh, hi," she says.

"I'm leaving my house now."

"What?"

I change it to "I'm on my way."

"Okay. I'll go downstairs," she says. This is the same routine each week at 9:40 am.

Today I take Ted's car and grab the cooler because I assume we're going to go to several stores. I also bring my own $5.00-off coupon for Cub Foods. I have a coupon for Q-tips and my Quaker granola bar coupon that Clara gave me a few weeks ago. Once again, I wonder if I'll turn out like Clara. We are different in so many ways; yet, I see so many similarities and wonder if she was like me five decades ago. The thought encourages me to learn from Clara.

I arrive at Clara's building. She's waiting in her usual spot inside the lobby; I see her white hair through the window. I get out of the car and open the door to help her down the steps. She tells me that I need to go upstairs and get her list and a coupon for Green Giant vegetables that she left on her dining room table. I go park my car, take her key, and head up in the elevator.

Her apartment smells sour and it is nauseating. I quickly grab the list and coupon for Green Giant vegetables, lock the door, and go back down. We go to Rainbow first. In the car, I ask if anyone has asked her to Thanksgiving dinner. She says no, with a pause. Is she expecting me to ask her? I say, "You can have dinner with my family, but I'm not quite sure where we're having it yet." I lie, knowing quite well we will have it at my house. She says she likes to stay home and eat her own food. I tell her I understand, but really, I wonder if she knows I am only asking to be nice. I am relieved.

I decide not to do my own shopping today. Things seem to go more quickly when I can just focus on Clara. Today's haul is two bags of oranges for $5.00, $.48 for a bag of carrots, $.98 for yams, and three bananas, which she analyses for more than five minutes. As I watch her do this, I realize I have the same habit of analysis. I'm going to be just like her! Well, maybe not exactly.

We make our way over to the fish counter, and I see the same butcher we see each week. I make my same weekly request for the fattest piece of cod. I get the usual look and response from him, "They're all the same." *I know they're all the same, but do you not understand that I have to ask this? Otherwise Clara will get mad.* Next stop is for

cottage cheese and milk. Clara had seen an advertisement for sixty-four ounces of milk for $1.50. As usual, nothing is marked as on sale. Neither Clara nor I can figure out if sixty-four ounces is a half-gallon or not. I'm surprised that Clara doesn't know this.

We next stop in the canned vegetable aisle. She has the Green Giant vegetable coupon: four cans for $1.00. Clara has an entire cabinet filled with canned vegetables at home, many of which I assume are expired. Is she really saving $1.00? I think it may be a waste. She wants the four cans anyway. Then it's here we go again, back around to the fruits and vegetables for the $.98-per-pound apples.

We finally check out and I go get the car. When I pull up to get her, Clara fools me and is standing at a different door for pick up!

At Byerly's I drive up to the front; she gets huffy when I stop at the left side door instead of the right. The doors are right next to each other. She behaves like this every time I drop her at a door. I explain to her again that I cannot always drop her off exactly where she wants me to because I am sometimes blocking customers from crossing. I get her routine response: "Oh, all right."

After parking, I search the grocery store for her and find her at the customer service counter. She is buying stamps. Next stop is the bread—challah and Jewish rye, sliced and doubled bagged. We make our way to the kosher butcher to pick up her two turkey thighs. The butcher hands them to me, packaged with my name on it. I'm taken back when I see my name. I forgot that I had

given him mine. The package is quite heavy. Clara wants
to know how much they are. When she finds out they're
$25.00, she's not happy. She tells the butcher that she
wanted the smallest turkey legs and thighs. The butcher
tells her they *are* the smallest.

She's stuck with them. She says she can buy a whole
turkey for that price. I don't tell her that I ordered a
whole turkey from the co-op for $2.09 a pound and paid
half of what she did. We take a stroll around to see what
the cranberry sauce costs. It ends up being more than
what she wants to spend. She also complains about how
much they sell the prunes for. It's the same thing I always
hear: "Walgreens sells them for $3.00." We check out and
go back to her apartment.

During the car ride back I remind her that I won't be
able to take her shopping next week. She says Joy is going
to take her, but won't take her on Wednesday. Clara is
clearly frustrated by this. She thinks it's ridiculous that
she can't go on Wednesday. I stand up for Joy on this
one. Shopping on the Wednesday before Thanksgiving
at the grocery store? No way! I remind her that it will be
difficult with her in the scooter and the crowds of people.
She also tells me she's getting her newspaper again. She
has cancelled and restarted her newspaper several times in
the past ten months all because they change the price so
frequently. Clara calls and argues with them, then cancels.

Today at her apartment she has me adjust the knob on
her washer. Then we clean out the lint from the trap in
her dryer. She thanks me and I am out of there quickly.

I leave to do my own grocery shopping at Cub Foods. I am excited to use my $5.00-off coupon. Years ago, I did such a good job shopping just once or twice a week. Now I can't seem to focus. I tend to be overwhelmed with too many groceries. I can only handle thinking about one or two meals at a time and then have to stop and go home. I have so much on my mind that I can't think straight. It frustrates me. Everyone always tells me I do too much. Maybe they're right.

Wednesday, November 30, 2011

I am dreading picking up Clara as I leave the house.

Clara is waiting for me in the lobby. She's wearing green knit pants and yellow slip-on shoes identical to the blue ones she has. The yellow ones have a big hole in them. She also has on white socks and her toes hang out of her shoes. I don't know how she's able to walk in those shoes. I'm always scared she's going to fall down. She has her regular blue coat on, and a green shirt that looks like it's a match to her pants.

In the car ride to the grocery store, she says she is on the "outs" with Valerie. Clara tells me that Valerie called and said she wanted to come over and visit. They were supposed to meet on Saturday, but then Valerie had to reschedule for Sunday at one o'clock. But *then* Valerie had to reschedule for 4:00 p.m. And *then* Valerie called at 4:00 p.m. and said she couldn't make it, but would come after work on Monday. Clara got mad and told Valerie her stomach was bothering her and that something was wrong with her eye, so she might as well not come over. Then

Clara hung up. Shortly after, either Valerie called back or Clara called Valerie and Valerie told Clara that she was being rude.

I'm sure Clara *was* being rude. I feel bad for Valerie. She's in a tough situation, too, sort of like I am. I don't know how she did it living next door to Clara and helping her for all those years. Clara also tells me that Joy took her shopping on Saturday.

At Rainbow Foods, Clara selects a bag of carrots, romaine lettuce, and a $.98 bag of onions. No fish today; she says it doesn't look good. At the bakery counter she gets angry with me and, with a harsh tone in her voice, tells me to move out of the way. Apparently, I am standing too close to the acrylic counter for her to see around me.

Ice cream is too much money today. She uses what I would consider foul language when she is disgusted by a price. Clara gets Total cereal today: six boxes for $9.99, plus her coupon and the savings from double-coupon Wednesday. At the checkout and after the clerk rings in her coupons, the cereal is free and she gets two coupons back for free milk and eggs.

I put coins in the Salvation Army's red kettle at the grocery store when we leave. I'm still curious to see if Clara will do the same, but she does not.

We return to her building. When Clara opens the door to her apartment, I gag from a weird, sour smell. It sells like someone has thrown up and not cleaned it up.

There seems to be no ventilation in her apartment; the air is stagnant. Clara tells me that the housekeeper didn't come last week because of Thanksgiving. I unpack Clara's groceries, and we clean the lint trap from her dryer. I sit and talk with her for about thirty to forty minutes. We talk about her family, mostly about her sister who lives out of state. I ask if her sister is still living, and Clara says she has no idea. *That's odd.* How can you not know if your sister is living? Is Clara really that isolated?

I look around her apartment at all the stuff she has, and I ask about it. Clara tells me she got many of the things during her travels. She has been to Europe, South America, Mexico, Singapore, Hong Kong, and Bangkok. She says that once she went on her first European trip, she was hooked and wanted to travel more after that, even though she always traveled alone. At first I am surprised to hear this, but after thinking about it, Clara traveling alone makes complete sense, knowing who she is.

She tells me about a tragic thing that happened on her Mexico trip. She was eating breakfast and heard a lot screaming. She ran outside to see what was going on. An elderly couple who were in their seventies had been sitting on the beach with their feet in the water. A big wave came by and swept them both out into the ocean. The woman got out okay. The man didn't get out and drowned, although they did find his body.

Clara said that was the worst thing that happened on any of her trips. I find listening to her interesting. For so long I only pictured Clara as an old woman who never experienced life, and yet she has story after story to tell.

And here I am wondering if I'm that old woman never experiencing life. With the tidbits of information she lets out sometimes, I wonder how much more she's actually done. She talks of her travels where "people buy the country, while I see the country." I'm guessing that means she didn't spend much money like the other people did.

I see the plants that Valerie gave her and comment on how good they look.

Clara says, "I have a question about your mom." She continues, "Is your mom kind of flighty?"

Laughing, I say, "Why do you ask?"

Clara says, "Remember the one time we were at Byerly's and your mom showed up without money?" She's referring to the night I took her to Byerly's after the fire in her building, when my mom called me because she had forgotten her purse and then stopped by our table and borrowed money from me for groceries and dinner. Clara wants to know what kind of person leaves without their purse, knowing they will need money for shopping. I have no answer for Clara. I know that if I do come up with some reason, Clara will just disagree.

Before I leave, I tell Clara that someday I'm going to write a book about our shopping. She laughs and says, "What's so interesting about shopping?" She then tells me that she has often thought of writing a book about "pricing." She has a catchy title for the name of her book, which includes the word "price." I'm not surprised that Clara is interested in writing a book about prices; her entire life revolves around finding the best prices on things.

The day ends up being a pretty nice one. I had a lot of anxiety before I saw Clara because, as always, I didn't know what to expect. Sometimes the smell, the attitude, and going a million different places annoys me. But I actually enjoyed our day today.

Wednesday, December 7, 2011

I call Clara from the lobby of her building and she tells
me to come up to her apartment and get the garage door
opener because she wants to be picked up in the garage.
I park and go up to her apartment, get the garage door
opener, and return to my car.

I drive into the garage and Clara comes shuffling
out the door in her black rubber galoshes, apparently
without wearing shoes inside of them. Without shoes, her
boots are so oversized she can barely walk. Her feet are
swimming in them, and she is unstable. She tells me that
she was not able to zip up her boots over her shoes, which
is why she just went with the boots and no shoes.

I think that she could fall and it would be my fault for
taking her out in the boots without shoes in the middle
of winter. I know it's wrong to take her out like this. I
suggest that I go back up to her apartment and get her
shoes. Clara says no. She seems a bit edgy today, wanting
to hurry and get her shopping done. I'm afraid to say no
and make her angry. With her blue jacket, she wears a
blue scarf, blue gloves, blue shirt, and blue pants. She has

dandruff on her blue jacket and she smells sour. I don't force the issue about her shoes.

Clara tells me that she is mad at Valerie because Valerie cancelled their plans to see each other. Clara sounds like a teenage girl talking about a boyfriend. Clara again tells me that her bank balance is too high. She looks at me for a reaction. I don't know what to say. She talks about investing some of it. However, she claims that when she calls her investment advisor, he never responds to her calls. Clara also tells me that she is tight with her money. I'm not comfortable talking about finances with Clara. I'm her volunteer, not her financial advisor! It's not appropriate for me to talk with her about this kind of stuff. Luckily the conversation ends when we arrive at Byerly's.

I drop her off at the door, watching her maneuver herself into the store in just her boots. In an effort to help stay balanced, she slides her feet instead of taking regular steps. I'm afraid she's going to fall over. I regret taking her out with no shoes.

When I meet her inside the bank, she is exchanging quarters in her purse for nickels and dimes. I can't understand this. *What is the need for nickels and dimes when you have quarters that do the same thing?* I guess this is just another one of those Clara things. Clara shuffles out of Byerly's, and we head to Rainbow Foods, where she once again shuffles in. I'm happy she rides a scooter in the store and not shuffle around in her boots. We do her usual shopping today without having any problems.

Once we're back at her apartment I see that she already has milk, as well as two dozen eggs. Why did she buy more?

That evening I tell Ted about Clara's boots with no shoes. He tells me I should never have taken her shopping with her boots like that, and that I should refuse to take her if she does it again. He reminds me that I don't need to be responsible for her falling.

Wednesday, December 14, 2011

I have my usual feelings of dread. I'm not sure if I feel this way today because I'm afraid that she will be dead, or if I'm just stressed over the amount of work it takes to take her shopping. It takes twenty minutes of calling from the lobby up to Clara's apartment before she answers. She wants me to pull into the garage to pick her up today. I assume that she is going to pull the no-shoes-in-the-boots thing again. I tell her that I will come up to her apartment first. I plan to help her get the boots on over the shoes. When I get to her apartment, I see that she has on her regular slip-on shoes, which is fine since the weather isn't that bad. I guess no boots today, then.

Before leaving, she tells me she is having a problem with the refrigerator freezing all of her food. I take a look and can't see any problems. I also don't see a separate control for the freezer and I'm cautious about moving any of the controls. The last thing I want is for her to be mad at me for messing up her refrigerator. I've already had enough problems with her TV.

On our way to the grocery store, we start talking about the refrigerator, and she gets angry. What she says sometimes really bothers me; she says things that I would never want to repeat. Clara has difficulty using mild tones in her voice when speaking about certain subjects. As I try to get out of the car to help her, she angrily says, "Get out." It's so strange the way she is. It's hard to describe. She's kind of mean and aggressive, I guess. Sometimes she doesn't say things loud, but just gives a stern, cold stare or mutters a quiet, mean comment. I'm used to her personality now.

Clara wants to go to Byerly's, Cub, and Rainbow today. I tell her that I have a one o'clock dentist appointment, and that we can go to Byerly's and Cub, but will not have time for Rainbow. Frankly, I'm happy about this. I'm tired of going to three different locations.

We make a quick stop at Byerly's for her to go to the bank. She asks me to go to the bakery there and get her the Jewish rye bread because she does not want to walk that far. I do as she asks and have to report back that Byerly's is out of rye bread today.

During our car ride to Cub she tells me that she cancelled and restarted her newspaper again. I wonder if the newspaper people are annoyed by this.

When we arrive at Cub, I again put coins in the Salvation Army's red kettle. I wonder how Clara will react. She watches me with her Clara stare. She can put coins in there; I know she has enough change in her purse to do this. She saves enough with all her coupons. What is she saving her money for? She doesn't spend it on herself or anyone else. Here she is, using me as a volunteer, and I would think that she could offer a few coins to the Salvation Army. It bothers me that she doesn't.

At Cub Foods, a woman comes up to me and tells me I'm doing a good thing. It's these gestures of kindness that keep me volunteering with Clara. I remember the first day I took Clara shopping. A woman stopped me then, too, to tell me it was a wonderful thing that I was doing. It seems like only yesterday. However, it was almost a year ago.

We both get a few groceries. She buys more cans of peaches and pears. These will be added to the many cans she already has. She buys more chicken thighs, even though her freezer is already stocked with chicken.

On our way home from the grocery store, she says her infamous, "I have a problem." As usual, I get nervous, because I never know what the problem will be. However, I have come to know that her problems are really not that bad. I think *she* thinks they are worse than what they really are. My hesitation is that if I can't fix whatever the problem is at the time, it becomes my problem, too.

It's exhausting taking on other people's problems. I know this, but I do it anyway. I wish I could say why I do this. Part of it is that I'm hypersensitive to everything that's around me. If I'm out walking through my neighborhood, for example, and I notice that the neighbors have not picked up their paper or mail, I take responsibility for it and call the neighbors to make sure everything is okay. Or I move their paper and mail to a secure location so no one notices that they may be out of town. I've also picked up lost mail and delivered it back to the post office.

When I see coyotes in the neighborhood, I call around and notify the neighbors. I have delivered several lost dogs to their owners, and have spent many hours looking for lost animals for people searching in our neighborhood.

I've helped stranded people. I've picked up several strangers and driven them to various locations when they were having difficulties with cars, or were lost or hurt. I watch and notice everything that people do. If people are sick, I recognize it right away and try to help. The list goes on. It's a daily battle for me to try *not* to notice things and *not* to get involved. It's draining on me. But I cannot stop.

Clara isn't happy when something doesn't work. However, she won't spend money to actually get the problem fixed. So this time—as usual—I say, "What's the problem?"

"My cleaning woman," she replies. By this point, I think she has been through several cleaning people. She continues, "My cleaning woman is short and stubby." Clara claims that the cleaning woman lies and doesn't come over when she says she is coming over. Clara tells me that the cleaning woman says she calls to get in, and she can't get in. I have to side with the cleaning woman on this one, because I have the same problem each week trying to get in. It took me twenty minutes of calling this morning before she answered and let me in. I must be more persistent than the cleaning person.

Clara thinks the cleaning woman is lying. Clara says that when the cleaning woman finally does get in to do the cleaning, her mood is ugly and belligerent. Clara tells her to clean the floor in the bathroom, and the kitchen, as well as dust. When she tells her to clean the cabinets, she only cleans them for two minutes. Clara claims she also doesn't do the floors, or cleans them for only a couple of minutes. Clara also says that she is only there for an hour and a half, but she is supposed to be there two hours or more.

I can only imagine the butting of heads that goes on between them. The cleaning woman is likely taken aback by Clara's behavior and retaliates by being mean to Clara. I'm never sure whom to blame when it comes to confrontations involving Clara. Regardless of who started the argument in this situation, Clara didn't like the way the cleaning woman was cleaning and finally told her to get out. After Clara tells me this story, she asks me if $21.00 an hour is too much to pay for cleaning. I tell her I used to pay $30.00 and more per hour per person. I clean my house myself now. I'm too neurotic to have other people in my house. They may bring in more germs.

Clara is clearly shocked by the $30.00 per person per hour. She, of course, questions me, and wants to know why I paid that much. I don't have an answer and divert to a new question.

I ask her about her annual association board meeting. She tells me she called one gentleman at the meeting a liar. I ask her why she called him that, and her response is matter of fact: "He is a liar."

"Why is he a liar?" I ask.

"He barged into my apartment and didn't even knock. He used the key and came in with two men. He said he didn't come in with two men. Then I called him a liar." People probably get so frustrated with her. I wonder if she had more patience when she was younger. I know she's getting older, but does that get her a free pass to say whatever she wants? I don't know, but it doesn't seem right.

When we get back to her apartment, I check her refrigerator again. I'm still not able to figure out the problem. I tell her to call someone to get it fixed. I know she won't. She knows I have an appointment and rushes me out. It's only 11:00 a.m., and my appointment is not until 1:00. Whenever I tell Clara that I need to be somewhere, she is very respectful of my need to leave on time. From the very first day that I met her, she has always been passionate about making sure I'm out the door by my requested time. I like that part of her, because it's similar to how I am. I'm sad thinking that I get upset with her at times. I have such mixed emotions. I feel sorry for her; yet, I am frustrated by her, too.

Thursday, December 22, 2011

Clara comes downstairs to meet me and tells me that she's having chest pains, feels weak, and overall is not well. She can't shop. I ask her if I can take her to the doctor. She tells me no. I worry about her. She always says no to my suggestions that she see a doctor and then tells me she's fine. It makes me wonder if, whether she talks about her mortality or not, she is actually scared to die. She is ninety-three years old; she must realize she is getting close.

Clara gives me her shopping list and tells me to go to Rainbow. I send her back upstairs to her apartment. I get her grocery shopping done quickly and then return to her building. I try to call her from the lobby, but get no answer. I continue to call for twenty to twenty-five minutes.

I'm getting more worried. I call the property manager's office. The manager is not there; however, I speak to someone in administration. The administrative person tries to be helpful and get a hold of the caretaker. However, I know that he's out, since I saw him leave earlier today. This is now extending into thirty minutes—like I have time for this!

I finally see the caretaker again walking through the hallway. I bang on the glass and he lets me in. The caretaker tells me that the cleaning woman has been here, too, and was unable to get a hold of Clara. I think that answers the question about whether the cleaning woman was lying about coming over to clean. We walk up to Clara's apartment, and the caretaker bangs on the door. Clara opens the door. I am so frustrated. I tell her I have been calling for thirty minutes, trying to get a hold of her. She says the phone didn't ring.

I call her telephone with my cell phone, and her telephone rings just fine. The volume of the TV is just too loud. I wish she would wear a hearing aid. I put her groceries away and get the lint trap from the dryer, which is now part of my usual routine.

Her apartment is getting so disgusting. Paper and plastic bags are piling up, and the dust is looking thick. The carpets have not been vacuumed and the sour smell is becoming more rancid. It's choking me. I won't take out her garbage. I just won't do it! If she is truly getting rid of her cleaning woman, I'm going to tell her she has to get a new one. Someone other than me has to check in with Clara and see if she's okay. The responsibility I've been taking on for Clara is probably a bit much. However, I don't see anyone else looking after her.

When I leave Clara's, I'm frustrated. I sit in my car and call Allison, Clara's social worker from the JFCS. I tell her that Clara really needs to be checked on, and must have a cleaning person.

I don't have time for this. Two of my kids have a Nordic ski meet, and the other has an intramural basketball game this afternoon. At the basketball game, I see my friend Judy whom I had seen while shopping with Clara last September. Judy is interested in knowing what I do for Clara since she does something similar for an elderly couple. I tell her about the shopping, appointments, errands, and the facial-hair trimming. I had told my friend Jan about the trimming, too. I don't tell my friends and family personal things about Clara; I know I have to keep information confidential regarding my relationship with her. However, talking about the hair trimming helps me cope with something that I found very unpleasant. Now when I see Jan and Judy, they poke fun at me, and tell me they know who to call when they start growing hair on their faces.

Friday, December 23, 2011

I call Clara on Friday to check on her. She asks, "Are you coming by here?"

I say, "I don't know. What do you need?"

"I can't reach the Total cereal you put on the top shelf."

I tell her that if I'm near her building, I will call and stop by.

She says, "Don't worry about it; I'll just eat oatmeal until next week."

"Okay," I say.

Do I need to feel guilty? A couple weeks earlier, she had me put six or seven boxes of Total cereal on an upper shelf. I knew she would not be able to reach them. However, I've learned that you don't argue with Clara; you just do as she says.

Monday, December 26, 2011

I call Clara to let her know that I'm going to stop by to get her cereal down from the upper cabinet. She asks me to stop at Byerly's and get her some challah and rye bread before I come over. I of course say yes. My daughter Margie comes with me and we go and get the breads. I am in luck; they have both kinds. I do the usual and ask the baker to slice and double bag Clara's bread.

Margie comes into Clara's apartment with me. While I'm getting the cereal down from the upper cabinet, Clara asks Margie if she visited the Duluth campus, and if she has decided on a college yet. Margie tells Clara she has not done either. Clara hands me an extra *Ladies Home Journal* magazine they sent her by mistake. She proceeds to tell us about the diarrhea she has had all day. I'm sure she ate something bad. Clara doesn't leave her apartment, and nobody comes in. I don't think she could have picked up a virus. She has a lot of old food in her refrigerator. I'm sure she ate something spoiled.

Wednesday, December 28, 2011

I call Clara from my house before I leave to pick her up.
She answers with her usual "Hallow?"

"Hi, Clara; it's Beth."

In an abrasive voice, she responds, "Where are you?"
She always sounds so angry.

I arrive at her building and she is wearing her blue coat
and stained green shirt, and she smells. She isn't breathing
well. She can't walk very well anymore, and can barely
get in the car. I have the feeling I won't be able to take
her out much longer. I can sense from Clara that she's
happy to get out of her apartment today, though. It's
important I take her out while she is able.

She wants to go to Cub and then the bank. I tell her
that's fine, but that maybe I should be shopping for her
since she doesn't seem well. She says, "We'll see."

She tells me that she got a check that states she needs
to cash it within thirty days. That's probably why she's
anxious to get out—to hurry and cash the check. I drop
her at the door at Byerly's so she can go to the bank. I

187

feel bad not walking her in. She is so hunched over and old looking. But it's difficult for me to walk her in and at the same time leave my car at the crosswalk unattended. I would need to drop her off, have her wait for me, and then walk her in. She would never wait for me. It's sad seeing her like this.

In the car on the way to Cub, I ask her if she's still cooking for herself. She replies, "Oh yeah." I'm glad to hear this.

At Cub she gets tomatoes, potatoes, a large bag of carrots, strawberries, chicken thighs, and ice cream. She selects the tricolor ice cream that she likes. The ice cream is, of course, on sale.

After shopping, I offer to take her garbage and recycling downstairs in her building, but she doesn't want me to. She has to go to the bathroom and she wants me out. She has me put away her groceries quickly, and rushes me out the door. I'm sure she wants her privacy.

Thursday, December 29, 2011

I'm having so many irregular heartbeats these days. I have to go to the doctor and get several tests. I wonder if it's the stress with Clara. I have mixed feelings about everything. I'm starting to feel sad for her, thinking about who would even be at her funeral and what her obituary will say. It's strange that I think about this. I'm worried about her being in her apartment alone and struggling more and more.

I'm journaling my notes from my Dictaphone and I hear a meow from my cat. It reminds me that I actually have a life of my own outside of Clara. I started journaling early on in our relationship, knowing we had something special between us. I started dictating our happenings because I had been too busy to write. Last week was a scare for me. I thought I had erased my recorded notes. When I checked my Dictaphone, there was no record of my long hours of voice recording. I started to panic. Luckily, Ted figured out that I just had the recorder on a different setting than I normally use. Losing my audio dictation would have been devastating. I have dictated so much about my time with Clara over the past year. It means a lot to me.

Wednesday, January 4, 2012

Clara needs to go to her pacemaker appointment. I pick her up at 8:30 a.m. and take her to the hospital. She is moving very slowly, and her balance is terrible. Her breathing is labored. I figure they will check her out at her appointment to make sure she's okay. I don't think she even knows that she can't walk very well. She is so determined. She even walks determined.

We stop at Byerly's after her appointment and I help Clara out of the car. She is very heavy. It's not that she weighs a lot; it's just that she's a bigger woman and she's like deadweight when I hold her. It's strange that she's so heavy when she appears to be thin. She pulls very hard on me as she tries to get out of the car. She's too heavy. I lose my balance and begin to fall. I accidentally hit her in the head with my hand. It isn't a bad hit, but it is a hit. I feel terrible. It does not seem to faze Clara, though.

I silently ask myself once again whether I should be taking her out on my own. Today shows how difficult it's becoming to get her in and out of the car. I'm going to contact the JFCS to let them know she needs more help—more help than I can provide to her.

Does Clara not understand that helping her physically is hard for someone my size? She really needs a special attendant to help her if she wants to go out.

We go to the bank and then Rainbow for her usual grocery shopping. In the car, I ask her about her pacemaker appointment. She says they told her one of the leads is not working properly. The doctors are just going to keep an eye on it. Maybe the lead not working has something to do with her difficult breathing. Her body seems to be wearing down.

Monday & Tuesday, January 9 & 10, 2012

I call Clara all day Monday, trying to get a hold of her to see how she's doing. I don't get an answer. I leave a message for the caretaker and don't hear back from him. I call her again Tuesday morning and she answers the phone. Apparently, she just didn't hear the phone ringing. She says she's fine, but tells me she wants me to do her grocery shopping again, without her.

Wednesday, January 11, 2012

When I get to her apartment, she is in her dirty robe, which has stains all over it. I ask how she's doing and she says, "Not so well," and that she is very weak. She cannot open the dryer to get her laundry out of the machine, so I take care of it and put it on her bed. It actually looks like she has a fitted sheet on her bed today. I've never seen a fitted sheet on her bed before, just the mattress pad. She has the fitted sheet with the mattress pad that she uses as a blanket.

We go over her list. First Byerly's to get challah, then to Walgreens to get her prunes, then to Rainbow.

Her TV is not working . . . again. This time there's no picture at all. The screen says "no signal." I try to push buttons and fix it, but it looks like there's truly no signal. I tell her that it's possibly the antenna that's causing the problem. She tells me that she called a few stores to ask about it. They also told her that it's probably her antenna. She said she called her caretaker. He hasn't called her back. Hopefully, tomorrow she will get some answers. She is sitting in her chair doing nothing. No TV—which is her life. She does have the newspaper, but how many times can you read the same paper? I take her list and shop for her.

Prunes are $3.00 per package. The coupon Clara has given me is expired and Walgreens won't take it. Clara said that at Rainbow, cod would be $6.00 a pound on sale; however, it is not on sale. I call her and get her lake trout for $7.99 instead. She also wants me to get two half-gallons of milk or one full gallon, whichever is cheaper. She tells me that the half-gallons are on sale. So I have to figure out which will be the better deal. Of course, there's nothing stating the milk is on sale. So I ask a gentleman who works at Rainbow and he says, "Gosh; someone else asked me that today, too, but they aren't on sale." I know if I go back to Clara's apartment and tell her the milk wasn't on sale, she'll be mad.

I put the groceries on the conveyer and go over to the customer service desk to ask about the milk. The clerk looks it up and sure enough, two half-gallons of milk are on sale for $3.00. A clerk has to go get me the two half-gallons. I feel bad because the woman in line behind me has to wait.

It's stressful to grocery shop for Clara even when she's not with me. I know I have to follow her prices and coupons. I have to call her several times to confirm an item, and when they don't have what she says is on sale, I have to look for people who work there and ask questions. It's a lot of work, and it's irritating. I'm not sure if I'm irritated at myself or at Clara; probably both. Admittedly, shopping with Clara has made me a frugal shopper. I definitely think before I buy now. At least when I'm shopping for her on my own, I don't worrying about her falling down. It seems all the people at our regular stores know I'm shopping for her, so they're kind when I have to get things corrected or ask a lot of questions.

I get back to Clara's apartment and put her groceries away. She already has several cans of peaches in her cabinet. Now she has more. She wants to give me $20.00 for gas. I struggle with this. She will get mad if I don't take it. I don't know how to feel. I do a lot of driving for her, going to several different stores and appointments, etc., almost every time we go out. Maybe I shouldn't feel bad about taking gas money.

I add up the three receipts and I tell her to check my adding. She always checks, even if I don't tell her to. Of course, I'm off by a dollar. I hate when this happens. It's the prunes. They cost $9.00. However, when I was adding, I wrote down $10.00 because when I looked at the receipt, I saw "$10.00" printed there. It turns out that that was the amount I gave to pay the bill. I'm frustrated that I made this mistake.

I feel like I'm being judged, and that I need to do things correctly. I'm not sure why Clara makes me feel this way. I don't want Clara to ever think I'm trying to take money from her. I just make mistakes when it comes to math. It's my dyslexia. I have never claimed to be good at math. It's good she checks. I'm good at grocery shopping, not math.

Clara continues to talk about having too much money in her checking account. I tell her to talk to her banker about investing some of it. She says no. She doesn't want to invest there. She says that it's best to diversify. She asks me if I invest in stocks. I tell her no. Today she also asks me about Margie's decision on college, like she does every week. She still can't understand why Margie would go away and spend money when she can live at home while attending college.

Before I leave, Clara pays me back with a check. I keep my receipts. I don't want people to ever think that she's giving me money.

Tuesday, January 17, 2012

I call Clara to let her know that I can't shop on Wednesday this week. We agree on Thursday instead. She tells me it's okay because she isn't going to go out anyway; I will need to do the shopping for her. I then get a call from Allison, the JFCS social worker. Apparently, Clara needs a whole list of cleaning supplies. I'm so frustrated!

I ask Allison why the cleaning woman doesn't just give the list to Clara. Why are they calling me? I know Clara will get mad when I bring the list. I think Allison called Clara and tried to give her the list, but Clara couldn't hear. I call Clara and have to shout into the phone, as usual. I try to tell her that Allison called me with a list of cleaning supplies. Clara, of course, gets huffy and wants to know why they didn't call her.

Why didn't the cleaning woman just give her a list when she was there last? Why do I have to be in the middle of this?

Thursday, January 19, 2012

I get up to Clara's apartment. She isn't doing well. She's tired, and says it's her heart. I tell her it's time to see a doctor, but she refuses to go. She's not eating very much anymore. She still has no signal on her TV. I'm trying to help her fix it; she wants me to call a repair person. How can I call a repair person when I'm not sure if the problem is with the TV or the antenna? I ask her who she called, and she says she called the manager of the building. I try to call him, too.

I'm so frustrated. I'm having trouble figuring out what the problem is with her TV. Her remote doesn't work, either. I think she may need new batteries again. I tell her this and she's clearly not happy. Clara is sitting in her blue-and-white-striped chair, eating her Total cereal; she's angry about my battery comment and starts choking. She is spitting up her food. I don't understand why she's so worked up just because I tell her she may need batteries for her remote! I think it's the entire TV situation that's making her upset.

After thirty minutes of me fiddling with the TV and listening to Clara rant and choke, she finally tells me that she already called the management company of her building about the issue. I call the management company myself and find out there's a problem with the antenna on the building. Apparently, they told Clara that yes, there's a problem with the building's antenna. Had Clara been clear about what she knew, I wouldn't have wasted all that time trying to get the TV to work.

Before leaving, I go over the list of cleaning supplies that Allison gave me. I look under Clara's sink and find three of the five things the cleaning woman says she needs, and Clara won't let me buy the others. Clara wants to ask the cleaning woman what she needs herself. Clara's toilets are horrible. If the cleaning products cost more than a dollar, she won't pay for it. I wonder if not having the right cleaning supplies is part of the reason the cleaning woman is having a hard time. I can't ask Clara this. I know that she'll just get mad.

After shopping, I bring Clara's groceries to her apartment and put them away. We sit and talk while waiting for her laundry to finish so I can help her with it. She tells me she won't use a hearing aid because a friend told her they don't work. She also says she won't use a walker. Clara tells me about her cataract surgery. She says one of her eyes works great, but the other doesn't work because she refuses to have surgery on it.

Her first surgery had gone fine; however, the service she hired to drop her off after the surgery just dropped her off downstairs and didn't help her up to her apartment. She couldn't get up the steep steps on her own, especially not after eye surgery. She only had one eye working, and was tired and dizzy from the anesthesia they had given her. She had to drag herself up the stairs holding on to the railing, and barely made it to her apartment.

The next day she went back for her follow-up visit, and when they took the bandage off her arm, she had a large fat pocket, as Clara describes it, on her arm. It was in the spot where she'd had an IV. She asked the doctor what it was, exactly. The doctor said he didn't know.

Years later, she still has the fat pocket. She is so upset by what happened with the first surgery that she doesn't want to have another.

Clara starts reading the obituaries while I'm there and asks me if I know a particular person because they were Jewish. I ask her what I should do if I find that she has died. She tells me that she has a burial spot in Superior. "Just get me to the Jewish morgue," she says.

Wednesday, January 25, 2012

Clara's TV still doesn't work, and she is infuriated. I'm sure she's been calling the building manager nonstop. She tells me she has lost a lot of weight. She is so frail. I don't know how she continues to get around, but she does. She hasn't been eating much and what she does eat goes right through her. I tell her I would like to take her to the doctor. Yelling at me, she says, "I DON'T NEED A DOCTOR; I NEED A LAWYER." She is enraged and wants me to call the attorney general regarding her TV problem. She is obviously very frustrated and wants something done. Her TV is her lifeline. I know she's not feeling well because of the fact that her TV isn't working. She's been sitting in her apartment for almost three weeks without a TV.

Clara is angry and depressed about her TV. She spends every hour of the day sitting in her blue-and-white-striped chair doing nothing. It looks as though she's just wasting away. I'm angry and frustrated, too. I don't need this extra stress. I have enough of my own stress with my job and family.

I call the management company of Clara's building to discuss the situation regarding the antenna. I speak to one gentleman who says he will talk to the manager of Clara's building. I have the phone number of this person, so I call him myself, too. He doesn't answer, so I leave him a message. Clara says he won't call me back. I call the management company again and speak to a woman this time. She says she's going to talk to the building manager's supervisor. Clara next insists I go knock on the caretaker's door. I knock, but he doesn't answer. I didn't expect him to, though, because I think he may be out of town.

She hands me her shopping list and tells me to go to Rainbow:

Tomatoes
Avocados
Bananas
Romaine lettuce
Cottage cheese

She also asks me to go to Walgreens for Breyers ice cream because it's on sale: two cartons for $6.49. She wants the triflavor again.

I'm at Rainbow and have to call Clara because the cottage cheese she wants is not on sale. She tells me not to buy it.

Next stop is Walgreens. I leave my phone in my car while I run in to get the Breyers ice cream. I miss the call from the building manager! I call him back and he doesn't answer. I want this TV problem fixed for Clara. I'm very frustrated.

After Walgreens I stop at the Dollar Store to pick up toilet bowl cleaner. This is one of the items Clara doesn't have that the cleaning person requested. The cleaner is $1.88. How can Clara argue with that price? If she won't pay for it, I'll just leave it with the other cleaning supplies. Her toilet is gross; she needs the cleaner.

I return back to Clara's apartment. Surprisingly, she doesn't argue about the toilet cleaner. She writes me a check for the groceries and the cleaner.

Clara asks me to get her mail from her box in the lobby. She also asks me to throw away her garbage. I'm not sure where to take it. I'm not sure exactly why I don't ask her. I go down to the garage expecting it to be there. I only see the recycling bin. It's funny; I begin to agonize over whether or not to just bring her garbage home with me. I can't figure out where to throw it. Little do I know there is a garbage chute down the hall from her apartment. And in the garage—around the corner from the large recycling bin—is a large door for the garbage thrown down the chute. You can toss large garbage bags that don't fit down the chute in the bin through this door.

Because I don't find the garbage bin, though, I just toss her garbage in the recycling bin. It's obvious that it's only recycling; however, I don't know what else to do. I can't go back to Clara's apartment and ask her where the garbage goes. She will give me that Clara look. And I can only imagine what she would say. I don't know why I'm afraid of her.

Over the week I make several phone calls about her television. I finally figure out the correct story. The antenna on the roof blew over during the windstorm a few weeks ago. The association won't pay to fix it because most of the residents have cable and no need for the antenna on the building. The antenna only affects a few people who still have regular TV. Clara has regular TV and needs the antenna.

That evening, Ted and I talk about the antenna issue and he suggests I bring her the antenna that he had made for our roof about three years ago. He made it with wood boards and hanger wire. I remember when he put it up on our roof. Our daughters and I protested. It looked awful. We made him take it down.

I agree that it might work for Clara. Ted cuts the boards down so that the antenna will not be so big in Clara's living room.

Wednesday, February 1, 2012

I call Clara to let her know that I'm leaving my house. She sounds tired and tells me she doesn't want to go out today. I tell her that I'm coming over there to set up an antenna for her TV.

I bring the antenna to Clara's and hook it up. The TV works perfectly! It seems to work even better than before. Clara is happy; she finally has her TV back. The antenna is big and not very attractive, but Clara doesn't mind, as long as her TV works.

I leave forgetting to tell her about the association's decision concerning the building's antenna. Because I can't speak with her on the phone because she can't hear, I will have to make an extra stop back at her apartment this week. I don't want her to keep calling the property manager's office and bugging them. She's kind of abrasive, and I'm sure she must be upsetting someone.

Saturday, February 4, 2012

I stop by Clara's to explain that the association won't pay for the antenna to be fixed. Clara has no interest in talking to me. She says, "Be quiet; a show is coming on." She just wants to watch TV. I tell her I'm only going to stay for two minutes to explain the issue. She won't listen. I try to tell her that unless she pays for cable TV, she is stuck with the antenna. She just complains about the building manager, blaming the antenna issue on him. She is very bitter. However, I believe she understands the issue now and will hopefully let it go. Before I leave, she has me move the antenna. It had fallen behind the couch. She wants it behind the curtain, near the sliding door to her deck. I tell her that I will not put it behind the curtain, but I will lean it against the wall.

Wednesday, February 8, 2012

Clara has me go to Byerly's to make a deposit in the bank, and of all things she asks me to check her addition. *Wow; she trusts me to check that?* She knows I'm not good with math. She has five checks and is off by one cent. This time it isn't my error. I catch hers! That's a change.

I get her challah at Byerly's. Then I'm off to Cub Foods for blueberries, peaches, eggs, ice cream, Total cereal, and some other miscellaneous items.

At the checkout counter, I get a coupon for free milk. I'm sure Clara knows that I will be coming home with this coupon. That's probably why she sent me to Cub today.

After I finish grocery shopping, I return to her apartment and put her groceries away. She says to me, "Did you get me a gallon of milk?"

"What? No; you didn't ask me to get you milk."

"I just tried the milk I have, and it's sour. Can you go back and get me the free gallon of milk with the coupon?"

Are you kidding me? As usual, I oblige. Why can't I just say no?

Off I go back to Cub Foods to get the free gallon of milk. This is taking up my time. She should have told me before. I'm not happy! While I wait in the checkout line, I notice that I cannot use the coupon at the time of sale. Clara must have known this. She is a coupon user extraordinaire. I wonder if she tricked me, knowing that I would have to return to Cub for a separate sale to use the coupon for the milk. I return again to her apartment with the milk and she asks me to empty her dishwasher. It takes me a while, since I need to ask her where everything goes.

Clara is having difficulty breathing. I really want to bring her to the doctor, and suggest that I take her. She refuses to go. I say to her that maybe it's her heart, because she keeps complaining that she's tired and winded. Her response is, "I'm old; what are they going to do?"

I think she just wants to be left alone. She has no appetite. Her body is wearing down. I'm conflicted about whether or not I should force her to see a doctor. I know she will get angry with me if I push the issue.

Clara writes me a check. She can barely write. Her hand shakes terribly. She can't even tear off the check from the book anymore. Things are getting so hard for her. I tell Clara we've been together over a year now. She is so surprised it's been that long. It almost looks as if she has tears in her eyes. Clara tells me that Allison is leaving the JFCS and will not be her social worker anymore. I knew this because I had gotten a call from Allison, too.

"I don't know what I would do without you," she says. It takes everything I have to hold back tears. Despite all the frustration I feel, I wonder what I would do without Clara. I know her time is coming soon, and I'm not sure if I'm ready for it, regardless of what I tell myself.

She did not have her TV on today. Usually when I say, "I'll see you next week," she is so engrossed in her TV that she hardly acknowledges my leaving. However, today is different. When I tell her I will see her next week, there is so much sadness in her eyes, and she just stares.

It's hard for me to see such sadness in her. I feel so bad for her. It's been a stressful and draining day.

Wednesday, February 15, 2012

Clara is crabby and depressed. I try to convince her to go to the doctor so they can check her pacemaker. She gets all mad, saying, "No. I don't want to be bothered." I tell her that maybe she needs more help and I suggest she have someone come over a few days a week to help. This makes her mad and she again says no. Then she comments, "I don't want to go to a nursing home because I don't want to do what everybody else does. I like my independence." Her comment doesn't surprise me. She is sad and depressed and she's just sitting there. She doesn't watch as much TV as she used to. She doesn't like to talk much anymore, either. She has lost ten more pounds and has no real appetite. I offer to do her laundry. She just doesn't want anything done.

I'm not sure she even knows what she wants. She is obviously uncomfortable and unhappy. I tell her I feel sad for her that she is sitting all alone. She gets mad again. It's interesting; any empathy toward her makes her upset. As sad as it sounds, I think she just wants to die. She's so tired. I feel bad for her. It would be horrible for her to go into a nursing home. I'm going to notify the JFCS about her health. I can't let her sit here helpless. Her TV is still going on at two in the morning. I write down the TV brand so I can search the Internet and try to figure out how to correct the problem.

Clara tells me her sister passed away, and that on Sunday she received several calls from relatives about it. I remember asking her a few months ago if her sister was still alive. She had told me that she did not know. I wonder if it was a surprise for her to hear of her sister's passing.

Clara tells me that a cousin asked if she needed anything: groceries, supplies, anything. She thought that was nice of him to ask, but told him no.

Clara hands me her shopping list for Rainbow. The list is covered in phlegm, and I get it on my hand. I am grossed out and want to vomit. I hold my hand stiffly away from my body and calmly excuse myself and go to the kitchen to wash my hands; she of course has no soap. I quietly take the spray cleaner that's in the cabinet under the sink and spray my hands. As well as being completely grossed out, I'm angry that I have to spray chemicals on my hands.

I come back to the living room and she gives me the Clara look. I wonder if she can see who I really am. Does she have any idea about my worries about germs? Does she know that I constantly worry about spoiled food? Does she know that I'd wash my hands a thousand times if I could? She continues to cough up phlegm. Again, I decide to call the JFCS and discuss Clara's frailness and her need for more help. I struggle with calling the JFCS, knowing she'll get mad at me. However, I also can't let her go on much longer without more help. I'm very conflicted.

I think she's at the end. But in certain ways she is still so strong, and this amazes me. I know she must have done everything for herself years ago. She always lived on her own and never had to depend on anyone until recently. She struggles because she doesn't want to depend on anyone. However, for her to survive, she has to.

I take her list and go to Rainbow. Although she did not ask me, I decide to make a stop at Cub Foods and get her peaches because I know she likes them. When I get back, she says, "Had I known you were going to Cub Foods, I would have had you get me a couple things there."

After I put the groceries away I sit down to talk to Clara for a few minutes. I tell her I'm worried about her and I think she needs more help. Clara gets visibly angry and she responds, "You're getting too involved."

Are you kidding me? I'm getting too involved? What kind of response is that? What have we been doing for the past year? I'm not sure if I'm going to cry or get angry at her. I let my feeling go and rephrase what I want to say. "When I signed up with the JFCS to be a volunteer, I made a commitment to you. I have the responsibility to make sure you are okay." She nods and says she understands. I then tell her that if she gets to the point where she feels she can't be on her own, she should tell me. I'll help her do something about it when the time comes. Clara nods and replies yes.

I know that some days are good and others are more difficult for Clara. I realize that I still can't cross any boundaries with her. I tell her I understand that she doesn't want to be bothered, and that I won't bother her. She promises me she will let me know if she's not okay. I guess I'm just going to have to respect her wishes and let it go. When I leave today, she seems okay.

She will be extremely upset with me if I cross the boundary and contact the JFCS regarding her. However, I think it's important to let them know what's going on. I'll send an email and try to do it in a way that won't upset Clara—or at least so she doesn't find out. In general, she seems fine. She can get around her apartment fine. She is still cooking and eating—maybe not a lot, but still, she makes what she wants, when she wants it. She also continues to write checks and pay bills. We'll see how it goes.

I go back to Rainbow to do my own grocery shopping. Like Clara, I try to spend less money. She's a good example of how to save money. While I shop I think about the not-so-nice comment she made about me getting too involved. It makes me feel bad. I've been her volunteer for an entire year now. It makes me feel sad that she would think I'm being too pushy when I hardly said anything other than, "I'm worried about you, and I think you may need some extra help." Tears fill my eyes.

I'm having so many irregular heartbeats again that I can hardly stand it. It's really getting to me. Clara gets so frustrated at times and makes me feel like she's mad at me.

Maybe it's just me feeling this way. Maybe I take things too personally.

Tuesday, February 21, 2012

Last night I had a dream that Clara died.

In the dream, Clara wants to go see a play. To get to the play, we have to climb stadium bleachers. The structure is like a mountain. We have to climb very high and for a long time. I keep wondering how she's going to do it. But she does it and gets to the top of the bleachers to watch the show. She is so excited about the show. She loves it. She even sings along. But people all around me are angry with me for making her climb to the top.

On the way home from the play, we're on a bus. Clara and I sit in the front row on the right, near the door. People all around us are angry with me. They keep telling me that I shouldn't have taken her to the play and up the bleachers because she is too old, and that she can't handle something like that.

While we're on the bus, Clara's heart starts bothering her. She is dying. I hold her in my arms, telling her it's going to be okay. She starts telling me things about anorexia. I continue to hold her, and she dies in my arms on the bus. Everyone is angry with me because I took her to the show. I try to tell them that she really enjoyed the show. Then my daughter Margie is suddenly there. She says, "She was going to die anyway."

Margie and I both tell everyone that Clara enjoyed her life until the end. Everyone gets off the bus while I wait for the medical examiners. When they arrive, they take off her clothes to prepare her for burial. They leave her on the bus with no clothes on, and this really bothers me.

I woke up when my alarm went off.

I call Clara to make sure she's okay. She's fine.

Wednesday, February 22, 2012

I call Clara before I leave my house. She sounds very weak and does not want to go shopping. I'll have to shop for her. I don't think she wants to go out, anyway, since it recently snowed. It has been a very mild winter. My kids haven't been very happy because there hasn't been enough snow for the Nordic ski season.

I arrive at her apartment and go over her shopping list. She seems peppier today than she was last week. She has probably been eating better and has more strength—not as depressed. She asks me how I'm doing. I know that when she asks me this, she is feeling better. It's interesting that I've gotten to know her so well. I ask her how she's feeling and she says her stomach is bothering her a little. I ask her if she threw up and she tells me she hasn't, but she feels like she would like to. She gives me a long list for Rainbow, which includes fish, and then tells me to go to Walgreens for the ice cream. It sounds like she's getting her appetite back.

Shopping at Rainbow is frustrating, as usual. The lettuce isn't marked $.75 as Clara is expecting. Of course, I have to go find someone to ask. I find out that the $.75 lettuce was only on the two-day sale—Sunday and Monday—for Presidents' Day. Does Clara know this, but still wants me to try, hoping Rainbow makes a mistake and gives her the price, or does she just not review the ads properly? Sometimes I think she's just testing to see if she can get away with things. I have to call Clara and go over the fact that the lettuce is not on sale. It's the same thing we always do.

"Clara, do you still want the lettuce?"

"How much is it?"

"Eighty-nine cents."

"Does it look good?" she asks.

I'm shouting in the phone and the customers look at me as if I'm crazy. Once I confirm what she wants, I go to find the smoked salmon package she has asked for. Of course, there's no smoked salmon. The same thing happens again when I get to the canned tomato section. She wants the Rolled Gold tomatoes that were also just on the two-day Presidents' Day sale. I have to call her again. She says she saw that when she rechecked the ads.

Rainbow doesn't have the rye bread she wants. I call to let her know before I go to check out. She asks me if they have Jewish rye. I tell her no. She asks me if they have any rye bread, and I tell her no. I'm away from the bakery at this point and I'm not going back to look. At the checkout counter, I realize I have forgotten her Cascade dishwasher detergent and have to go back and get it. I leave the groceries at the counter with the cashier. When I get to the Cascade and look for the regular kind she's requesting, it again becomes complicated. They only have the "Shield Guard" version and some others. None say just regular. Without calling her, I select what I think is closest to regular. It's on sale. How can she argue with that?

I decide to swing by Byerly's on my way back to her apartment, crossing my fingers that Byerly's will have the rye bread. They do. I go to Walgreens, too, and get her the two cartons of Breyers ice cream. I think the total savings on the ice cream ends up being about $3.00, which is likely what the gas cost to drive to all the stores. I think I might say something to Clara about it.

Wednesday, February 29, 2012

A big snow day! We have a few trees down in our yard.
Our arborvitae that we tried to save from a storm last
winter is now crushed by the heavy snow again. It's also a
late start for the schools today because of the snow. I have
to be home with my kids this morning and today is my
shopping day with Clara. I need to tell Clara that I will be
late. I try calling her several times and cannot get a hold
of her. I get a busy signal. I call the building manager to
see if there's a way I can get in when I get there. I'm a bit
concerned she hasn't called me. It's our regular shopping
day. She always calls me when I'm not there when she
expects me. Even if I'm five minutes late, I get the usual,
"Where are you?"

I'm concerned and get ready to head over to Clara's.
I plan to ask her if she has a box of old-looking candles.
Margie is working on an art project and needs several
boxes of vintage candles. It's hard to find these types of
candles. I'm hoping Clara will have a box. I've never
asked Clara for anything before so I'm a bit nervous about
it.

I go into the lobby of Clara's building and exchange calls with the building's management company, trying to figure out a way to get into the building. While I wait to get a contact, a very nice elderly man passes by the door with his groceries in the red grocery cart from downstairs, and he lets me in. I explain to him who I am and that I can't get a hold of Clara.

I bang on Clara's door and, of course, she's there, just fine. I tell her that her phone is off the hook. She goes in the bedroom and starts repeating into the receiver, "Hello, hello, hello." I can hear her voice coming through the phone that's off the hook in the dining room. I put the phone back on the receiver for her, and remind her that she has to set the phone back on the receiver correctly or it will not hang up. She gives me the irritated Clara look, like I don't know what I'm talking about.

She gives me her shopping list and makes me rewrite it, because she says I can't read her handwriting. I can read it fine, but I rewrite it anyway. She has already put her laundry into the washing machine. So I put the soap in and start the wash.

I'm able to get all of her food at Rainbow. The total is about $21.00. She saves a lot of money with the way she shops for sales and uses coupons. My grocery bills are at least $250.00 a week. When I return to her apartment and put away her groceries, I ask her if she has any extra boxes of candles that she is willing to give me for Margie's AP ceramics project at school. It seems that anytime I mention school to Clara, she's all in favor! She has one very old box that she hands me. Clara's candles are dried out. I wonder how old they are. There's a lot of dust on the box.

As I leave today, Clara says, "Maybe next week you can help me with something." Oh! I get nervous when she has that tone in her voice and look on her face. I never know what her requests will be. She pushed it with the shaving of the beard.

I ask her what she needs help with. "Maybe you will be nice enough and help me clip my toenails." *What? You have to be kidding me.* There's no way I'm going to do that. I shaved her beard once; I don't think I can clip her toenails. Where do I draw the line? This is insane; she needs a nurse. Regardless of what I'm thinking, I tell her maybe. I also tell her that I might not be strong enough if her nails are really hard. I'm not kidding, I'm sure her nails are nasty and tough. I wonder when she last cut her nails. I don't think I can do it!

On the way home, I think about this toenail-clipping thing. I've shaved her beard and gotten her phlegm all over me; maybe I can clip her toenails. I try to see the humor in all of this. I'll have to prepare myself mentally. Can any nails be worse than mine were? I had such terrible and painful nails about twenty years ago that I had all ten permanently removed. All those years of running ruined my toenails. I'm sure mine were in much worse shape than Clara's can be. I have a week to think about Clara's toenails. I just won't eat before I cut her nails, since I might vomit. I'll wear my rubber gloves. She'll think I'm nuts—or I guess more nuts than she already thinks I am.

Wednesday, March 7, 2012

It's 8:53 a.m. and I call Clara. She can barely speak. I ask
her if I'm going shopping for her today and she says yes.
I tell her I will be there at 9:30. She sounds exhausted.
Today is the day I'm supposed to clip her toenails. I'm not
sure if that will happen or not. Just in case, I'm prepared
with my gloves.

I arrive at Clara's and she's the same: tired, without much
of an appetite. She still seems okay, though. She talks a
lot today and tells me that her nephew came to visit her.
She asked him to do something about the issue she had
with the association regarding her TV problem. She keeps
talking about the fact she didn't have a TV for a month.
She keeps saying the board lied to her. She goes on and
on about it. I don't think the board lied to her. I think
she just didn't understand what was going on with the
antenna. Apparently, her nephew told her to forget about
it. I'm glad he told her that. She will hopefully let this
issue go now.

The antenna I gave her has fallen down, so she doesn't want to turn on her TV. I pick up the antenna and set it back against the wall, and she turns on her TV. I take her laundry out of the dryer, put it on her bed, and we clean the lint out of the trap. I go down to the lobby and get her mail and mail a letter for her. I then go to Byerly's to make a deposit for her and get her some challah. Then it's on to Rainbow for tomatoes, green beans, two heads of lettuce, milk, eggs (coupon), and cottage cheese (coupon). The total for the week is $15.00.

I get everything back to her apartment and unload her groceries. She has so many rotten lettuce heads in her refrigerator. I throw out her garbage, as she requests. Her apartment stinks like rotten food. I gag from it. I hate the smell. I still can't figure out what smells so bad. Even after the garbage goes out, it smells.

I sit and talk with Clara for a bit and she tells me that at one point she almost got married, but it never worked out. She knew he wasn't the right person. She never found the right person, although she dated several people. I comment that she's so independent, she can take care of herself.

She responds, "Yes, but it would have been nice to lean on somebody. It got lonely at times."

Wow; what a surprising statement from Clara. She has been strong her whole life. I guess I just imagined she didn't think she needed anyone. I can picture how hard it would be to be alone for so long.

Lucky for me, she forgot about the toenail clipping today.

Tuesday, March 13, 2012

I email the JFCS this morning and inform them that Clara's mobility and her health are not good, and that Clara needs extra help. I call Clara to tell her that I'm leaving my house and will be over soon. She tells me she has to go out and visit two banks. I'm concerned—I'm not sure how this is going to go. She hasn't been out in a long time—at least a couple months. I question her ability to walk and get around outside her apartment.

I get to Clara's and she again tells me that she has too much money in her bank account. She wants to get half the money from one bank and deposit it into two other banks. I ask her if she has accounts at the two other banks that she wants to go to. She says she does not.

I understand that she doesn't want to keep all of her money in one bank, and I'm willing to help. However, it will most likely be an all-day event to go to two banks, set up accounts, and transfer the money. I don't like getting involved in her financial stuff. I just agree to take her where she wants to go. I tell her a lot of people have their money in one bank. She doesn't think that's right. She feels that you should spread the money around to different banks in case something happens to the one bank that has all your money. I see what she's saying, but at the same time it seems like a little paranoia and a lot of work.

Our talking must have worn her out, because she then tells me that she doesn't feel well enough to go out. I'm very relieved about this. I assure her that her money will be fine in the bank where it currently is. And I promise that when she feels well enough, I will take her to the bank. She gives me her shopping list and coupons.

I go to Rainbow to get Hebrew National kosher hot dogs, tomatoes, tomato sauce, grapes, two avocados, and ice cream. Clara has a coupon for $5.00 off when you buy eight cans of tomato sauce, and two packages of the hot dogs. Unfortunately, they do not have the kind of tomato sauce that Clara wants. I call her and shout this information into the phone. She tells me to just get one package of hot dogs, no cans of sauce, and to skip the coupon.

I bring Clara's groceries back and unpack them. I sit on the couch next to her blue-and-white-striped chair, where she is sitting. I suggest that maybe she should contact one of those transportation services for seniors to help her get to appointments. She just shakes her head no. She will have to, because it's getting to the point where I really can't take her out anymore.

She asks me to call the community center and find out about the tax preparation services for this year. She tells me that she tried to call them, but could not hear or understand what they were saying over the phone. I call the community center and get the information. We decide that next Wednesday I will take her to the community center so she can get her taxes done.

I take out her trash and do a load of laundry for her, too. She pays me cash for her groceries. She counts out $12.33 in exact change. I leave quickly, because she has to go to the bathroom. She doesn't like when I'm there when she has to go to the bathroom.

After I return home, Clara calls to tell me her blue light to her TV is not working. I know she's talking about her converter box light. I ask her if it needs batteries and she responds, "No, it's broken." I say okay, and tell her that I will be near her building around twelve thirty on Thursday afternoon and I can stop then and have a look. In a very terse voice she says, "Well, what am I going to do? I won't have a TV tonight." She is obviously upset that I won't come over right now and fix the problem.

Thursday, March 15, 2012

I stop by Clara's to check her TV. Clara tells me that the remote fell to the floor from her chair and that the remote is now broken. I check the remote and it looks fine. I doubt that it would have broken from a fall like that. Her chair is not very high and the room is carpeted. I have batteries with me, because last time I checked her remote, it was a little slow to respond. I picked up the batteries on my way to Clara's, assuming that they would fix the problem. I didn't want to get to Clara's, leave, go buy new batteries, and then go back. I put the new batteries in the remote and it works. She asks me how I knew it was the batteries. I tell her I just knew.

Wednesday, March 21, 2012

I pick Clara up at 8:00 a.m. to go to the community center to get her taxes done. This will be the first time she's been out since December. I meet her in the lobby of her building. She is sitting down and breathing heavily. It must have taken all her strength to get down to the lobby. She is huffing and puffing, and I can see her chest going up and down; she has to rest for a bit before we leave.

I get her in the car. We drive to the community center; she gets out of my car and immediately sits on the bench outside by the door. I park the car, then walk her in and sit her down. It's been a year since we have last done this. My expectation is that it will be the same as last year. There's already a waiting list of fourteen people. I put Clara's name on the list—number fifteen—and it's 8:15 a.m. I grab the form and fill it out for her as best I can. I then have her look it over and fill in the rest.

I can't sit down because there aren't any seats available, so I walk around and look at all the postings on the wall. After about thirty minutes of pacing around, I decide to take advantage of the extra time and go do some grocery shopping for Clara. She gives me her house keys and motions for me to come close to her. She says in my ear that she left the door open. She still can't lock her door because her hands are too weak. She thinks she's whispering; however, she's actually talking loud enough for everyone to hear.

I first go to Rainbow to get fish and milk. I need to bring the items to her apartment so they don't spoil sitting in my car. Once everything is in her refrigerator, I head back to the community center to check on Clara. She still hasn't met with an accountant yet. It is 9:45 a.m. She then tells me she needs bread at Byerly's. So off I go to Byerly's. At Byerly's I get her challah and a few things for myself. When I get back to the community center, Clara is still waiting. It's after 11:00 a.m., so I go out and run more errands for myself.

I get back to the community center at noon. Clara is finally in the room, meeting with the accountant. She waited four hours to meet with an accountant who will do her taxes free of charge. I make conversation with the volunteer at the desk, as I had done last year. The volunteer tells me about her mother who is Clara's age. She speaks of the care her mother needs.

Watching the people come in late and be turned away is similar to what happened last year. A man in his seventies, hunched over, walks down the hall shouting, "Excuse me, excuse me, excuse me," at the same time he's asking people where he needs to sign up. He is the last one to make it on the list. I help the volunteer explain to the latecomers that they can only accept the first twenty or so people.

As I wait for Clara, I glance into the room where she is meeting with the accountant. I see her stand, so I go over to see what's going on. The room has approximately three or four accountants and there are several tables filled with customers meeting with the accountants working on taxes. Clara leans over the table, looking angry. She's making that frightening look on her face that I've seen so frequently over the past year and a half. I know that angry face well. She crinkles her eyes and she exposes her teeth. She doesn't have the strength to yell anymore as she did with the pharmacist at Walgreens last fall.

She is speaking loudly in a very bitter voice. "I don't know what's taking so long; he doesn't know what he's doing. I had the other guy last year."

I start to get anxious, too. I go into the room and say to her, "Clara, calm down; it takes time to get the taxes done. They have to recheck to make sure they do things correctly. They also have one of the other accountants in the room check it."

Clara won't take her stuff out of the bag again for the accountant to recheck. I tell her she has to take it out of the bag. Clara is angry at the fact that another person has to recheck her tax return. I know she's acting this way because she's not well and because she's drained from sitting here for five hours. It would have been better for her to pay an accountant to do this. Someone could have either come to her apartment to do her taxes, or she could

233

have dropped them off to an accountant. Either way, she wouldn't have had to sit here. Clara's tax returns take a little over an hour to prepare. It's the same as last year, but her patience level is just not the same anymore. I don't remember her getting so worked up last year. She is so cranky.

When I drop her off at her home, she pays me for the groceries. She goes to her chair and I'm reminded how she will spend the rest of her day. I don't offer to do anything around her apartment. I've been exchanging emails with the JFCS about how Clara is doing. They tell me I'm not allowed to do certain things for her, such as the laundry, pushing her in a wheelchair, and taking out garbage. The biggest thing that I am *not* supposed to do is go shopping without her.

I had no idea! I can't take her out anymore; she is just too frail. I really agonize over this. I know she needs help. The JFCS told me there are other services she can apply for to help her with some of these things. I emailed the JFCS back to let them know Clara and I have been shopping together for over a year now and it's only recently that her health began failing. I would feel horrible telling her that I can't shop for her. I know everything about her groceries. Clara will just get into an argument with someone she doesn't know. This person will bring home the wrong thing, not get the right price, not use a coupon, choose too small a head of lettuce, not pick the tomatoes that she likes, or get the wrong size fish. The list goes on.

I can shop for her with my eyes closed now. It still scares me to think what would happen if I made a mistake with her shopping list. I know what happened to Valerie when she brought home a nectarine instead of a peach by mistake. I've seen Clara in action and I never want to be on the other end of an argument with her. I can't believe that I'm this tormented with her shopping; what is wrong with me?

I explain to Clara what the JCFS has told me, that I cannot be doing all the same things for her anymore, and that she will need more help. I tell Clara that the JFCS has other services that she can apply for. She just needs to call them. I think she is too tired to listen. I leave her apartment quickly. It's been a long morning, and I need to go. The consolation is that I got through another tax season with Clara—yeah!

Wednesday, March 28, 2012

I call Clara at 8:45 a.m. and there's no answer. I leave my house at 9:30 to go to Clara's. Upon entering the lobby of her building, I hear banging. There must be some construction being done today. I don't like construction dust.

I call Clara from the lobby and still there's no answer. I'm concerned; however, Clara does not always hear the phone, so I try to stay calm. I finally call another resident in the building to let me in. I explain that I'm Clara's volunteer through the JFCS, I can't get a hold of her, and I need to get in. While I'm waiting to be let in, I keep hearing the banging; it's kind of like hammering. I look around and don't see any construction workers.

I finally get in and go up the elevator to Clara's floor. I walk down the hallway to her door and see her newspaper sitting outside her door. The door is ajar. Oh no! I immediately know something is wrong. The two most important things in Clara's life are her newspaper and her TV. She would never leave her newspaper outside the door. I push the door slightly open and yell

"Clara!" The pounding is much louder now.

I open the door further and hear a muffled voice. I find Clara flat on her back, lying on the kitchen floor; she's pounding on the floor with her hand. It's frightening to see her like this. She looks terribly pale and is unable to move herself. She can't speak, but can only produce a small muffled sound. She motions for me to help her get up. I tell her I cannot do that. I don't even touch her. She may have broken or fractured something in her body. I'm not going to risk moving her.

I ask her if she's okay, and she replies yes in a faint voice. I tell her to hang on and that I'm going to call 911 to get help. I call 911 and describe the situation. As I'm on the phone with 911, I keep my eyes on Clara. Her nightgown is drawn up and I'm in shock to see how horribly thin and frail she really is.

After I get off the phone with 911, I adjust Clara's nightgown, covering her. Clara then asks me to go to her bedroom and get her watch and ring. After a frantic search for the watch and ring, I find them in a little glass ring dish that I had overlooked on her nightstand. Once I get those to her, she puts them on. I ask how she fell and how long she's been on the floor like this. In a muffled, weak voice, she tells me that she fell the day before while she was going for the newspaper. I can't believe it! She's been lying here for twenty-four hours, banging on the floor. She must have been yelling at one point, too. Where were her neighbors? Could no one in the building hear the banging? Her door was open. I could hear the banging from the lobby.

The fire department arrives first. Clara asks for water, but the firemen won't give it to her. I can tell she's dehydrated. They want to wait until the paramedics get there, in case she needs an IV or further tests at the hospital.

The paramedics come next and ask me questions about Clara and her medications. I tell them about her upcoming pacemaker appointment and that the doctors are watching one of the leads. I also let them know that she takes medication for her thyroid. I hope I've covered it all. They ask Clara several questions. However, she can't understand what the paramedics are saying, so I have to step in and repeat the questions to her in a loud voice that she can hear. The paramedics determine she didn't have a stroke. I didn't think she'd had a stroke. She is alert and aware. There is blood on the floor; she may have lost a tooth during the fall. The paramedics finally allow her a small bit of water. She needs it terribly.

After they give her water, she coughs up blood. But her blood pressure and oxygen are good. Clara doesn't seem to be injured in any way, and she's cognizant of everything that is going on. When the paramedics get her upright in a chair, she asks them to check the oven to make sure there's nothing in there. It's interesting that she's thinking about this right now; same old Clara! The paramedics want her to go to the hospital in an ambulance. Clara agrees.

Clara tells me to go grab the blue bag that's on the chair in her bedroom and to put a robe and nightgown from her closet into the bag. She's also concerned about the newspaper being out. I had already put it inside her apartment, knowing she would be thinking about the paper. I check her apartment, turn off the lights, and make sure there are no appliances on. I lock the door behind me and hand Clara her purse, bag, and keys. I should have grabbed her prescription. Hopefully, the hospital will have record of it.

Clara is too weak and cannot be on her own anymore. I will insist that she have help. I call her cousin Joy who is listed as Clara's emergency contact, to let her know what happened. Joy suggests that someone call her nephew Lyle, also.

I'm determined to get Clara the assistance she needs. I call the JFCS and let them know what happened to Clara. I also let them know that Joy had said to contact Clara's nephew. They email me an incident report to fill out.

Thursday, March 29, 2012

I go to the hospital to visit Clara. I park several blocks away so I don't have to pay for parking. It's a nice day and I don't mind the walk. Clara is in the ICU. I walk into her room while they're trying to give her some sherbet and liquids. She is gurgling and seems to have a lot of phlegm. She looks the same as she did yesterday. They're trying to feed her and all she does is cough up phlegm. It's awful to see her like this. She can barely eat.

She tells me they aren't treating her well at the hospital and she says if they don't give her food soon, she's leaving. I tell her it wouldn't be a good idea for her to leave. She says she can leave whenever she wants. Obviously, she can't. No doctor will let her go home in her condition. She tells me she's going to go to the Sholom Home Assisted Living. She then asks me to move the little table in front of her so she can drink the liquid that's in a cup on the table. She has her blue purse right next to her in the bed. She has a cute little ponytail in her hair. Her hospital room smells sour. I speak to the person trying to feed her. The nurse tells me they're going to need to do some tests to find out why Clara has so much phlegm.

Clara has no strength. I'm glad that she finally admits she needs to go to assisted living. She wants me to take her keys, go get her newspapers, and hold onto them. I tell her I can't do that. But I tell her that I will call the property manager of the building to see if someone could take care of this for her. I'm trying not to overstep my boundaries. I don't think I should be taking her keys and getting newspapers from her building. Also, it will be too hard for me to get there every day. I call the building manager and we speak about the newspapers. He tells me he'll figure something out and he'll bring it up at the board meeting this week to see if anyone can pick up her newspapers.

I email the JFCS to update them on Clara's condition and to let them know that I have visited her. I also mention that I am taking care of the newspaper issue.

Saturday, March 31, 2012

I go to the hospital at 7:30 a.m. and park a few blocks away again so I don't have to pay for parking. I know how Clara likes to save money; it's obviously rubbing off on me. Paying for parking just doesn't seem right when I can walk.

Clara is even more weak and tired than before. Clara introduces me to the hospital staff as her friend. This is nice to hear. I've always wondered how she would address our relationship. The nurse tells me that Clara is being stubborn and won't take any of the medications. She will only take her thyroid medication. Knowing Clara as well as I do, I'm not surprised by this.

The doctors and nurses are trying to figure out why Clara keeps aspirating. However, Clara doesn't seem interested in finding out what's wrong with her. It's almost as if she doesn't want to get better. Clara looks sickly. They take her blood pressure; it's 110/96. They want to repeat the blood pressure test. The cuff and pressure around her arm must really hurt her, because she winces. She doesn't have the strength to fight back anymore, though. It's strange to see her like this.

Up until the past few months, she has been strong and able to disagree and argue with people. I wonder what she was like before I met her. She is ninety-three years old. She must have been very strong when she was younger. Even a year ago she would be hooting and hollering at the people working at the hospital. I can see she wants to tell the nurse to stop with the blood pressure tests, but she does not have the strength. Again, she tells me that she is going to Sholom. She's not hooked up to any IVs and she's not eating. She can't eat.

I call the hospital that evening to check with the nurses to see how Clara is. They tell me that she will be transferred to Sholom in the morning.

Sunday, April 1, 2012

I call Sholom to verify that Clara has been moved to their
facility. They say she's there.

I go over to Sholom in the morning to visit her. Clara
is in a double room; a curtain is between her and a
roommate. Clara is sleeping and breathing heavily. The
TV is on in her room.

The only two things of Clara's in the room are her
purse and her blue overnight bag that I grabbed when she
left her apartment for the hospital. I talk to Clara's nurse,
and then wake Clara so I can talk to her. I ask Clara if she
needs me to go to her apartment and get her a few of her
things. She says yes. I also ask her if I should get rid of any
spoiled food in her refrigerator when I'm there. I know
that she has a lot of rotting food and I want to make sure
it gets tossed out before it smells worse than it already
does in there. She agrees. I tell her I will talk to the social
worker at Sholom tomorrow and see if it would be okay
for me to do this.

Monday, April 2, 2012

I get up early and email the director of the social services at Sholom. I tell her who I am and ask her what I need to do to help Clara.

At 1:00 p.m. I go to Sholom. Before I get to Clara's room, I meet the director of social services. She tells me that she has received my email, but has not had a chance to respond. I tell her I'm going to visit with Clara. The director tells me she will let Clara's social worker, Melanie, know that I'm in the building.

Clara is sitting up in her bed. The speech therapist is here, trying to get Clara to eat. There is strange-looking food on Clara's tray—it looks like mashed potatoes, rare meat, and something else I don't recognize. I'm happy to see Clara sitting up, trying to eat. Clara says, "The food is terrible." The speech therapist leaves the room and brings back some tuna salad for Clara; Clara seems to like it better. It was nice of the therapist to get Clara something different to eat.

Melanie comes into the room to talk to Clara about a plan for her care. I talk to Melanie about the need to get some items from Clara's apartment. Melanie has a form that she's going to ask Clara if she would be willing to sign. The form gives Sholom the okay to discuss with me plans relating to Clara. I wasn't expecting something like this; however, I guess I'm not surprised, either, there isn't anyone else to advocate for Clara.

I'm happy to help Clara in any way I can. I'm curious to see if she will even sign the form. From what Clara said a few weeks back, I'm getting too involved; I'm not sure how involved she really wants me to be right now. While the social worker is in the room, I get Clara's keys out of her purse. I'm uncomfortable going into Clara's purse. I leave Clara while she's eating lunch.

It's a crazy busy day for me. I race around and pick up my kids from school and bring them to lacrosse. I then go to Clara's apartment. The apartment is worse than I ever expected.

I first go to her closet and get her two bathrobes, four pairs of pants, and four shirts. I look for shoes for her and see that they're all beaten up and worn out. I select a pair that I think will be okay: her usual slip-on kind. I then go to the kitchen.

I see that there are pots and pans on the counters and stove. When I take the tops off the pans, the smell is so putrid I almost vomit. There is rotting food in every pan, and I have never seen anything so disgusting. Is this why her apartment smells so bad? I clean all the pots, pans, and dishes, and put them in the dishwasher. I start the dishwasher. Next is the refrigerator. It's just as gross as the pots and pans. She has several jars of saved liquids that look like old water from a dirty toilet. I'm retching. I toss the gross-looking liquids without opening the jars, as well as all the rotten food I can find.

Wednesday, April 4, 2012

Joy calls me to let me know that she visited Clara. Clara mentioned to Joy that she needs help with some financial stuff. I obviously cannot be doing financial stuff for or with Clara. I wonder what she needs help with. I better ask Clara so I can find someone to help her.

Thursday, April 5, 2012

I go to Sholom to check on Clara. As I step off the elevator onto Clara's floor, a resident yells to me, "Hey, you! Push me into the dining hall." I walk over to the resident and then look at the nurse's station. The nurse smiles and waves me off.

When I get to Clara's room, a nurse is getting Clara ready to go to the shower. Clara and I talk briefly before she leaves the room. She gives me five checks she wants me to deposit into the bank. She also wants me to go get her anklet socks, grab her mail, and pick up her estimated tax documents so she can make her estimated tax payments. Her body may be very weak, but her mind is still very strong. This must be the financial stuff that Clara was talking about with Joy.

We also talk about the fact that Medicare will pay for one hundred days of nursing care if Clara participates in therapy. This information was given to me by Clara's social worker. Apparently, Clara is not cooperating with the therapists. I ask Clara if she wants to stay at Sholom. She tells me she does. I tell her that I want her to stay here, too, because she cannot take care of herself in her apartment anymore. I tell Clara that she needs to cooperate with the therapists and Melanie, her social worker.

"The Sholom staff is here to help you. You need to listen and work with them."

Clara nods.

I leave and go to the bank. The bank is closed. I then go to Clara's apartment. She told me where to look for the tax information—on the dresser in her bedroom. I find her state estimated tax documents, but not her federal ones. While I'm still in her bedroom, I grab the anklets from the dresser drawer. She also wants me to look around for any bills that need to be paid. I check the dining room table, her buffet, and her side table in the living room. I do not see any bills. I quickly water her plants with a jar from the cabinet. On my way out, I grab her mail from the lobby. I leave and go back to the bank and make her deposit. I then head back to Sholom to bring her the items she has requested.

When I get to her room, she is getting her bedding changed. I speak to Clara again about making sure she cooperates with the Sholom staff.

Joy calls me to see if I've spoken with Clara about the financial stuff. I tell her that I have, and that Clara asked me to get her estimated tax information, locate any bills that need to be paid, and make a deposit for her. It's all taken care of. Joy then tells me that Clara wants to talk to me about her will and finding an attorney. *What?* Clara did not ask me about this when I saw her.

Joy and I agree that I cannot help Clara with this kind of thing, and we both decide to look for an attorney for Clara. I tell Joy that I will also talk to Clara's social worker at Sholom about it. Maybe they know of an attorney.

Saturday, April 7, 2012

I've been trying to visit (i.e., talk) with the resident parrot at Sholom. He doesn't seem too interested in me. I hear him talking as I walk down the hallway. However, when I approach his birdcage or talk to him, he is silent and stares at me though the corner of his eye. I think he's sizing me up. I had told my daughters about the parrot not talking to me. They suggested I try bobbing my head up and down when I talk to him. I look around to make sure no one is watching me; I'm embarrassed. I begin to bob my head up and down as I speak to the parrot. The parrot is still uninterested.

I am so frustrated with Clara right now. I don't know why she refuses to participate in therapy at Sholom. It must be one of two reasons: either Clara thinks that she will have to pay for therapy, or she doesn't want people bothering her. It's likely both.

When I see Clara, she hands me some papers to throw away. One of the papers is a letter from the hospital. It's a letter written by a doctor; Clara had signed the letter. The letter is about her treatment while she was in the hospital a couple of days ago. The letter specifically states that Clara refused treatment. Clara said no to blood work, but yes to antibiotics. She said she would accept resuscitation. All else is no. It is dated and signed by Clara. I'm glad she's able to make these decisions for herself.

Clara is being her usual crabby self today. She tries to speak, but it's very hard for her. It's becoming increasingly difficult for her to communicate. She shakes her head yes or no to my questions. It's frustrating, because I'm trying to help her. Now that I know she didn't accept any tests in the hospital, and most likely will not accept any at Sholom, I won't know if there's something wrong with her physically. I suspect that there is, and that her health has been in decline for several months now. How can she be helped if she won't let anyone figure out what's wrong with her?

Clara is coughing up blood. She tells me she has tightness in her stomach. The nurse who puts Clara back in bed after she changes her sheets needs to use some kind of belt contraption to move Clara around. The belt helps so that they don't drop Clara and the person doing the lifting doesn't get injured. Clara gets angry about the straps. I tell her they have to use them. She doesn't listen to me. This does not surprise me.

Clara tells me the medicine they gave her left a bad taste in her mouth. She wants me to go to her apartment and get her association dues payment coupon book and property tax payment subs, and to look for her IRS payment stuff again. She then asks me if one of my relatives can do a will for her. *What?* I tell her no, that it's not appropriate because of my relationship with her. I ask her why she doesn't have a will at ninety-three.

She responds, "I do have a will, but it doesn't matter anymore."

What does that mean, it doesn't matter anymore? I ask her why she doesn't just call the attorney who did the will for her before. She tells me she doesn't like him. *Surprise, surprise. Does she ever like anyone?* I really hope that someone at Sholom can help her with this, because it cannot be me. She asks to look at her wallet in her purse. I hand her the purse and she checks her wallet to make sure everything is there. She gives the usual Clara nod of approval.

I go to Clara's apartment and find the property tax stuff, as well as the association coupon book. I still can't find her current IRS information, so I grab the most recent information that I can find, which is from 2010. I glance at her address book and debate whether or not to bring this to her. I know she's worried about having her things at Sholom. I think the address book is best left at the apartment.

I grab her mail on my way out. As I'm leaving, I notice her keys have "do not copy" written on them. It's not surprising. I wonder if she has ever given her keys to anyone before. From the way she behaves, it's as if she doesn't trust anyone or feels she is being cheated. I find it interesting that she actually trusts me enough to give me her keys and go get things from her apartment.

I get back to Sholom and sit with Clara and talk. We discuss her long-term plan, which includes the fact that she can't go home. She agrees. We talk about her preferences about assisted living versus nursing care. She says that she isn't sure she is well enough to be in assisted living. I ask if she can walk on her own. She tells me she cannot. I again explain to her that Medicare will pay for one hundred days of care, as long as she participates in therapy. She nods her head. I ask her why she doesn't want to do therapy. She doesn't give me an answer—just a blank stare. Again, I think there are two reasons. One, she thinks she has to pay, and two, she doesn't want to be bothered.

This must be so depressing for her. She sits here doing nothing. She doesn't even want to watch television when I offer to turn it on for her. I say to Clara, "You took care of yourself for almost ninety-three years; now you need to let people take care of you."

She nods.

I continue, "It's amazing that you had been able to take care for yourself for that long."

She again nods her head.

Monday, April 9, 2012

I am at Sholom and it is 8:45 a.m. I meet Melanie and we go upstairs to talk to Clara. We find Clara hunched over, asleep in a wheelchair in the dining hall. We wake her up. It's obvious she hasn't eaten very much. Clara says, "The food is sour." We wheel her back to her room.

Melanie talks with Clara about her long-term care. Clara expresses that she wants to stay at Sholom. Melanie talks with Clara about participating in therapy. Clara complains to Melanie about the therapy. She says she does not like the "mouth therapy." Clara must be talking about the speech therapy. Melanie again explains that Medicare will pay for one hundred days as long as Clara participates. Clara finally agrees to try the therapy.

Sholom puts Clara on a waiting list for a permanent room in the nursing facility, not on the wait-list for assisted living. Melanie tells Clara the monthly cost for nursing care and asks Clara if she can afford this. Clara nods and says yes. Melanie is also here to talk to Clara about transportation to her pacemaker appointment tomorrow. Clara writes a check to pay for the transportation and gives the check to Melanie. I'm glad Clara agrees to this transportation, because I'm not taking her.

I help Clara write checks for her other bills. I ask Melanie if she knows of an attorney that other residents at Sholom have worked with. She tells me that she doesn't know of any.

I go home and log onto the IRS website and print out an estimated tax payment form for Clara. I spend about an hour calling all my contacts, looking for an attorney for Clara. I know several; however, I want to find her someone I don't know. I think it's better this way. I don't want to be involved once I find her an attorney. This is Clara's deal, not mine.

I'm really struggling to find her someone who can meet sooner rather than later, though. Clara's cousin Joy is also helping look. A friend of mine finally calls me with a name and number. I call the attorney and set up an appointment for Clara to meet with the attorney on Thursday, April 19. I was really hoping to have him meet with Clara sooner than that. However, he's not able to.

I stop at Cub Foods and pick up a few roma tomatoes for Clara. She didn't ask me for them; however, they're her favorite food and I'm hoping it will cheer her up.

I head back to Sholom. I set the tomatoes on her table and let her know they're here if she wants them. She's happy to see the tomatoes and thanks me. I ask her if she wants me to bring her a box of Total cereal. She says no.

Clara must not be well if she doesn't want her Total.

I help her write the checks for her estimated federal income taxes, as well as her property taxes. I tell Clara about the meeting I set up for her to meet with an attorney about her will. I have a feeling Clara is not going to make it to the 19th, and I can see in her eyes that she feels the same way. I must find someone who can meet with her sooner. I don't know why I'm feeling anxious about this for her. She already has a will.

The fact that she said, "It doesn't matter anymore" makes me a bit worried for her. I don't want to ask her about it because it's none of my business. But I don't think she should be changing her will right now, if that's what she means. Her request seems strange. I'm sure other people think it's strange, too. I wish I could read her mind. I can't; however, I seem to always feel what she does. It is very peculiar; we are somehow connected emotionally. Maybe it's because of the time I've spent with her.

Tuesday, April 10, 2012

Melanie emails me to ask if I want to be part of another meeting she's having with Clara regarding Clara's long-term plan for care. I tell Melanie that if Clara wants me to be there, I'm happy to do so. Otherwise, I don't need to be there, because Clara is fine making her own care decisions. Melanie tells me Clara will be going into hospice.

Does hospice mean that she's dying?

I arrive at Sholom to see Clara, and it's obvious that her health is failing. She looks terrible and keeps complaining about her stomach hurting. I'm so freaked out about this! I'm totally stressed right now. I have so much going on; my brain is on overload. I have work, kids' school and sports stuff, and family things that I also need to take care of. I can hardly keep up with all that I'm doing. I'm frustrated by this situation with Clara. I'm caring for this woman I only met a year and a half ago. What am I doing?

Had Clara listened to me and gotten help, she might not be in this situation. Someone might have been in the apartment with her when she fell. Or she might not have fallen at all. *She is so stubborn!* I knew she wasn't well. I wanted her to see a doctor. She refused. Her stomach has been bothering her for a while. I'm sure there's something wrong with it. However, I'll never know, because she refuses any testing.

Apparently, Clara won't take her medicine. So I try to talk to Clara about taking it, but she says the medicine hurts her stomach and she doesn't want to take it. I tell Clara that Joy and I are still working on trying to find her an attorney who can meet with her sooner. While I visit Clara, the hospice social services director comes into Clara's room to discuss Clara's care. Because Clara is having a difficult time talking, I help the director understand what Clara is saying.

The director talks to Clara about the plan for hospice. I wonder if Clara knows what "hospice" means. They go over a list of available services from hospice, like volunteer visitors, massages, music, etc. Clara understands and decides on what services she wants. After the meeting, Clara asks me to call Valerie. Clara wants to see Valerie's dog. I leave Valerie a message. Joy calls and gives me the name of an attorney. This attorney may be able to meet with Clara sooner.

Wednesday, April 11, 2012

The breakfast they bring Clara looks very unappetizing. It's some kind of mushy cereal. I ask the nurse what the food is. She tells me it's cereal.

"It doesn't look like cereal," I say.

She says it's Passover and that the cereal is made from matzo meal. Oh no! I remember Clara telling me that she gets sick from matzo. Is this why Clara's stomach is hurting her? I tell the nurse that Clara should not be given any more food with matzo meal in it.

Clara's stomach pain and gas are obviously uncomfortable. It's awful to see her like this. I really wish I had known they were giving her matzo meal. I would have stopped them. However, I can't be angry, since the staff didn't know that Clara can't tolerate matzo meal and she didn't tell them, either.

Clara's liquids have to be thickened with a special thickener. Regular liquids go right into her lungs. All her liquids (water, apple juice, etc.) have thickener in them. Clara doesn't like the thickener. She won't drink. Her mouth is so dry. I try to encourage her to drink. She tells me she chokes when she drinks the thick liquids. Her ability to speak is progressively getting worse. I speak with Valerie about Clara. She tells me that she will visit Clara.

Friday, April 13, 2012

A social worker from Sholom gives me the name of an attorney. I call immediately and leave a message. He must sense the anxiety in my voice, because he calls me back right away. I explain the situation and he agrees to come out this afternoon. I'm relieved. I have this obsession with helping people. I also like to get things done efficiently and quickly and, most important, correctly. This is why I'm working so hard, trying to get this settled for Clara. I sense that Clara needs this, and I'm going to get it done for her.

I meet Clara's cousin Joy for the first time. She is at Sholom visiting Clara. I've often wondered about her and Clara's relationship. I know she has helped Clara with shopping because Clara has told me this. I can tell she cares for Clara and wants to be here to help.

I speak with Clara's nephew today. He sounds like a nice man. He is listed as her next of kin. He is checking to see how Clara is. It's hard for him to visit because he doesn't live in town.

I visit Clara and ask her if Valerie came by with her dog. Clara says that she did, and that the dog licked her. Clara seems very happy about seeing Valerie and her dog.

I tell Clara that an attorney will be here this afternoon to meet with her. She nods. I can see the pain in her eyes. She is absolutely miserable. Physically, she's the worst I've seen her. She passes gas in horrible pain. Her entire body thrusts when the gas passes through her. She seems to be self-conscious about it, too. I try to let her know it's okay, and that if it feels better to pass the gas, it doesn't bother me. Her entire body lifts up, and she groans. I feel bad for her.

She asks me to take off her watch and ring and put them in her wallet. I know she's not well because she never takes them off. The ring falls off her finger. She has lost so much weight. She is extremely frail. Her arms are so thin that they look like bones without skin. It's awful to see. She soils and urinates in her bed before she meets with the attorney. She has to be changed.

The nurses get Clara into a wheelchair and down to the conference room to meet with Larry, the attorney. I help Clara get situated at the conference table. Clara is picking at her nose. The oxygen tube has been irritating it. Joy is there, too, and hands Clara a tissue. Clara asks if I could go to her apartment and get the copy of her current will and give it to the attorney. I tell her that I'll take care of it.

I don't want to be in the room, so I leave. Clara doesn't want anyone in the room other than the attorney. As I leave, I look at Clara through the glass window of the conference room. It's too sad seeing her this way. She's hunched over the table. She has a blanket wrapped around her. I know that it takes every ounce of her energy to have this meeting. Whatever she's doing, it must be very important to her.

I go to Clara's apartment to look for her will. She said it would be on her buffet. I dig through several piles of paper and find three envelopes addressed to Clara from her previous attorney. I assume that her will is in one of these three envelopes. I drop the envelopes off at Larry's office. He tells me that Clara got too tired and was not able to finish the meeting, and that he will go back there on Sunday to finish.

Saturday, April 14, 2012

I can't begin to describe how miserable Clara is, lying in bed, unable to move without help. Her speech is failing. Her stomach gives her serious pain. She wets herself when I'm there. She's very aware and communicates with me. Clara and I have become so connected that I can understand her without her even speaking.

My inner voice keeps telling me to help Clara. Why do I always have this feeling that I have to help people? I reflect again that I've been this way my entire life, ever since I was a girl and felt the need to advocate for my siblings and be the peacekeeper in my family. I guess I shouldn't be surprised that I'm helping someone like Clara. But I am surprised at how close we've become, and how difficult it is for me to see her in such distress.

Clara is dying. There aren't many days left to complete her will. The attorney recommends that I be at the meeting tomorrow to help Clara. I want to support her, yet I also have so much frustration and hesitation. If she wanted to change her will, she should have done it when she was well, not when she's dying. Helping her do this is uncomfortable for me. I've helped Clara with so much over the past year and a half, but this goes way beyond. Clara wants things her way because that's the way she is. I have to support her. She should just be able to die without having to worry about her will. Why do I keep crying? I'm taking on her stress!

Sholom is doing a good job taking care of Clara. She has a lot of support. I think the staff is getting a sense of what Clara is like. She is stubborn and very persistent. When she needs the nurses, she pushes the call–light button continuously until someone shows up. It reminds me of when we were at the grocery store and she would push the "on" button over and over until the scooter would go. I keep bugging the staff with Clara's requests, too. I wonder what they think of me. *A mini-Clara, maybe?* My anxiety for Clara must make me act like her. Clara keeps wetting herself. I'm not sure if she is having bowel movements anymore. She's not really eating anymore. I'm now her friend, not just a volunteer. She needs me as a friend now.

Holding back my tears, I tell Clara I'm going to miss her. I say, "What am I going to do on Wednesdays?" I also tell her that I bet she didn't think she was going to meet someone like me. She stares at me with her Clara look. I wonder what she's thinking when she looks at me like this.

Sunday, April 15, 2012

Larry is here for the second meeting with Clara. He wants Clara to meet in the conference room again. I've come to Sholom early to help Clara get down to the conference room. She says she doesn't want to go, but wants to meet in her room instead. I tell her it's important that she meet with her attorney sitting up in the conference room, not lying in her bed in her room. She agrees and I have the nurses help her out of bed.

I wheel her downstairs and into the conference room where Larry is waiting. Larry has had a couple days to review Clara's current will. I am very nervous and hesitant to be in the room. I am about to be privy to very private information. However, I know Clara needs me. She has asked me to be here. And Larry says it would be a good idea that I be here to help her, too.

Clara sits in her chair, hunched over. Larry goes over what Clara is planning. She is willing her money and property to a fund for children. Wow! What an amazing thing for her to do with her money. Clara does not have any children of her own. But I do know how very special

children are to her. She had told me about her time
volunteering in the preschool.

Larry then asks Clara who she wants to have as the
personal representative of her estate. He tells Clara that
this is the person who will carry out the wishes stated in
the will. Clara looks at me, with her usual stare, lifts her
hand, and points her crooked finger at me. It's the same
finger I have watched push her TV button over and over.
It's also the same finger she used to point at her coupons
and push the scooter button; and most recently, the finger
I saw push the nurse's call button on her bed repeatedly.
*Oh no; this can't be happening. Why is she asking me? I've
only known her a year and a half. Does she really trust me that
much? Clara trusts no one. How can she be asking me this?*

I'm panicked! I look at Larry for guidance. We stare
at each other for a brief moment. Larry knows my story.
I'm just her volunteer. I wonder if he's as shocked as I am.
I look back at Clara with tears in my eyes. How can I say
no to her? She's dying, and she's asking me to make sure
that all of her money goes to a fund for children.

I nod my head and agree.

I cry to her about how I'm going to miss her and tell her
that I'm going to write a book about our time together.
She says, "I can't thank you enough." I tell her she
doesn't need to thank me. I promise her that I will do
things exactly the way she wants them done. I tell her she
needs to hang in there so she can sign the will.

Monday, April 16, 2012

Clara's nephew called me again to find out how to get a
hold of Clara. He hasn't been able to reach her. Joy also
called to check on her. Today Clara looks about the same
as yesterday. I tell her I talked with her nephew and he
may come see her. We read the paper together. I have the
nurses move her around several times. She needs changing
because she's wet herself. I have them get her something
to drink, too.

I tell her she needs to drink fluids to stay strong
for her meeting this afternoon with Larry. She is very
uncomfortable. Nothing makes her happy. She wants her
nails clipped. I have the nurse come in to clip them. The
nurse is a really nice man; he makes a funny comment
about how his three-year-old doesn't like it when he clips
her nails. I make a joke and tell Clara he's going to paint
her nails next. I guess she doesn't think it's funny, because
she says no and shakes her head.

A coworker calls me as I'm sitting with Clara. I turn
my back so I can talk with this person about work. At the
same time, Clara's oxygen tube comes out of her nose.

Out of the corner of my eye, I can see her struggling to adjust the tube. I put the phone down and hesitantly put her oxygen back in her nose as best I can. My anxieties are still such that I'm afraid to touch her. I have a fear of getting some horrible disease. She is picking at her nose again. Maybe the tube is uncomfortable.

Clara is slowly shutting down and her body isn't functioning well. She is incapacitated, wets herself, passes gas, and needs constant moving around so she doesn't get sore. It's awful to see her this way. I have done so much crying today. I cry again while speaking to Clara and tell her I'm going to miss her. I'm not sure why I keep crying. I wonder if anyone has ever cried over Clara. I don't think I'm crying because I'm sad. I think I'm just overwhelmed with everything that's happening. It's not unusual; I cry easily, and always have.

I think that Clara choosing to give away all of her money to charity is very philanthropic. I promise Clara that I will do everything exactly as she wants. Clara knows that I will. Clara has taught me so much about myself. Clara could have bought herself many comforts that would have made her life better in the end. However, she's chosen to live as if she has nothing and give her money away after her death. Thinking back on the time when I was frustrated with Clara for not putting coins in the Salvation Army red kettle, I feel bad for ever being upset with her. She was saving for her charity!

I was, and still am, concerned about being Clara's personal representative. I know I will do what she wants. It's the time that scares me. I voice my concerns to Larry. He says that getting through the estate process won't take too long, only about four to six months. I laugh. He says it as if it were no time at all. I know what's ahead of me, thinking about her apartment. Larry says I can pay myself for taking on this responsibility. Apparently, a personal representative can be paid from the estate. I wonder if Clara knows this. I tell Larry I will never pay myself. How can I take money away from an estate that has been left to a fund for children?

Larry says he can bring the will over to Clara to sign this afternoon. He tells me we need two witnesses for the signing. Larry tells me I can be a witness, since the personal representative is allowed to be one. I want to check this out with another attorney just to make sure he's correct.

I call a friend who is an attorney. My friend confirms with an estate attorney in her office that a personal representative can be a witness. After I get off the phone, I call a couple of my friends, and get a hold of my friend Tammi. Tammi knows about my volunteer time with Clara. Tammi is such a good friend; she agrees to come after work. I know that it won't be convenient for her because of the long drive to Sholom during rush hour. I feel bad asking her to do this. However, I want someone who knows me and my situation with Clara.

I meet Tammi in the lobby of Sholom. While we wait for Larry, I warn Tammi that Clara is very frail looking and that it might be difficult for her to see Clara. Tammi has recently lost her own grandma with whom she was extremely close. I know it will be hard for her to see Clara.

Larry arrives and we all go up to Clara's room. Tammi has tears in her eyes when she sees Clara. Clara is holding the will, following along as Larry reads it out loud. It reminds me of when she would scrutinize her receipts after grocery shopping. After Larry finishes reading and Clara reviews the will, she nods her head, and says yes.

Clara signs her will with Tammi and me as her witnesses.

Tuesday, April 17, 2012

I'm at Sholom for a brief meeting with Melanie and the head nurse. Clara doesn't want medication or therapy to make her comfortable. She refuses. She's not eating or drinking. We talk about a health-care directive. I call Larry and he says Clara has one; it just needs to be updated. Larry says he will do the documents and get them over to Clara to sign.

Clara is uncomfortable, and she needs moving. I adjust her oxygen and give her juice. The rabbi comes into Clara's room. She is a nice woman. She is with Sholom hospice, and has many questions for Clara about her family and friends. Clara cannot speak well, so the rabbi has Clara write answers to the questions on a piece of paper. Clara writes her dad's name, her mom's maiden name, and she writes her Hebrew name and those of her parents. Clara tells us that she wants a headstone like her parents'.

When the rabbi asks Clara if she wants a healing prayer, Clara responds no, along with the usual shake of her head. The rabbi and I step out into the hallway, and I tell her a bit about Clara.

After the rabbi leaves, and knowing I will be in charge of Clara's estate, I need to ask Clara a couple questions before she dies. I feel weird doing this. However, I know I will need this information.

"Clara, I need to know if you have a safety deposit box and where it is located."

Clara nods her head, and tells me where I can find the key. "It's in my purse."

I should have known this. Clara carries everything important in her purse. I ask again where the box is located. She tells me which bank. Interesting, this is not the bank she normally banks at. I have a hunch things will be a bit more complicated than I think.

I cry a lot throughout the day.

Larry calls midday to ask if I can meet with a woman from the foundation where Clara's fund will be to talk about the specifics of the fund. Larry feels we need to focus on where exactly Clara wants her money to go. Larry and I get a list from the foundation. The list covers items such as food, clothing, education (e.g., tuition to college and graduate school), and a couple of other miscellaneous programs. Without even asking Clara, I know exactly which programs she will select.

After we meet with the woman and get the list, Larry and I go to see Clara to discuss her options for distributions from her children's fund. Larry begins reading the list we have received from the foundation.

Clara is to answer yes or no to our questions about where she wants her funds to go.

Education is very important to Clara. When Larry gets to the questions about which colleges and universities students will be able to apply money from her fund toward, Clara—not surprisingly—selects the University of Minnesota. Larry then gives Clara a list of specific graduate school programs that students could also use money from her fund to pay for: law school, medical school, and dental school.

Clara stares directly at me with her Clara look—it's a look I will never forget. She knows my children are interested in attending graduate school. She firmly nods her head, and says yes to both medical school and law school. Without even speaking, she is giving me another lecture on colleges for my children. Clara's eyes have spoken to me before, and it's very apparent that they are speaking right now. Is this her way of telling me that if my kids select the U of M for graduate school, they, too, can apply to her fund for scholarships?

When Larry gets to the dental school question, Clara firmly shakes her head, saying no to money for students wanting to attend dental school. I laugh to myself, knowing that she was going to say no to this one. I don't know why; I just knew. Maybe it's her teeth? After the fund discussion, we move onto the health-care directive. Larry hands her the updated document. Clara reads it and crosses off one item. She then signs it.

After we're done, Larry looks at me and says, "She really knows what she's doing." Yes, she does! Clara's mind is sharp! Larry holds her hand and thanks her. Clara has that same blank stare on her face. I can't describe it. I wonder what goes through her mind when she has this look. It almost seems as though she doesn't know how to deal with closeness or people showing her empathy. When I cry she gives me the same "wonder look." I call it the "wonder look" because it's as if she's wondering how to respond.

I sit with Clara and I'm crying. She doesn't seem as restless anymore. She doesn't want anything to drink or eat. I hand her the newspaper. She reads the paper while I look at the *Good Housekeeping* magazine she has. I ask if she minds if I stay, or if she would rather I leave. She says she doesn't mind that I stay.

We talk about her Hebrew name and her parents again. I tell her I will go to Superior. I think she knows what I mean. I don't want to say, "When you die." She wets herself again and wants me to get the attendant. I leave the room to tell them. She continues to push the nurses' call button over and over.

I tell her I'll be back in the morning with her mail, and then we can pay her bills. She gives me a strange look; kind of like a blank stare, but different than her other stares. I have this feeling that tomorrow will be her last day.

I leave when the nurses come to change her. Clara looks peaceful.

Wednesday, April 18, 2012

It's 9:00 a.m. and I'm getting ready to go see Clara. My cell phone rings. Margie answers it and says to me, "I think Clara's dead, because it's Sholom." Margie tends to be a bit dramatic. I start to get shaky.

Margie hands me the phone. It's Melanie, Clara's social worker; she's heard Margie's comment and she chuckles. Somehow we both find humor in it. Clara hasn't passed away, but she has taken a turn for the worse. I know it's coming today. It is three weeks to the day that I found her lying on the floor in her kitchen. I drop the laundry and rush out the door.

When I get there, the nurse tells me that Clara is cold and clammy. When I see Clara, it's like looking at death. It almost looks like she's been prepared to look dead. She is lying on her back, with her hair slicked back. She is pale and stiff. Her eyes are sunken in and her jawbone is protruding. Her skin is extremely thin.

She knows I'm here because she motions to me to come over and wants me to help her get more comfortable. She can't speak, but is very aware of who I am and what is going on. I ask her if she's in pain; she shakes her head no. The past few weeks have been about trust. Clara had to trust me to understand her needs when she could not speak. How did I get to know this woman so well, and yet not really know much about her at all?

After Clara is adjusted and more comfortable, I move to sit on the bed next to her, trying to hold her hand, hoping to comfort her. Before today, the only times I have ever really touched Clara were when I helped her in and out of my car, and when we hugged on her birthday last summer. It's uncomfortable for me to hold her hand now, but I feel it needs to be done. She jerks and pulls her hand away. I'm not sure if it's because she doesn't want me holding her hand, or if it's a muscular reaction as her body shuts down. Is this just an expression of her personality? Her arms and hands are jerking a lot. She can't seem to help it.

After Clara pulls her hand away, I go to the chair that I have used the past few weeks during my visits. As usual, I reluctantly sit in it, neurotic about germs. I decide I need to write. I have no paper, so I grab one of Clara's newspapers. I can't use today's paper just in case she wants to read it. *Do I really think she is going to read today's paper?* I select the *Star Tribune*, dated Friday, April 13th. I know Clara won't be happy that I am using the newspaper for such a thing. However, I need to write. I have a red pen and begin to write in the margins of the paper.

Clara opens her eyes and looks up toward the ceiling, then she grabs the rail on her bed. I know she is dying. I wonder what brought me to this point. Is this all meant to be? It is all playing out in my head exactly as I thought it would; me sitting with Clara as she dies. Being left the duties of caring for her estate was always in the back of my mind, too. Did I create this situation, or did she? It's a thought that scares me, yet inspires me to live my life differently and make this relationship have some lasting meaning. It's weird that I'm writing about Clara dying. I number my writing sections on the newspaper because my writing is completely unorganized—all over the place and in no logical order.

As she looks up at the ceiling, it seems she is looking at something. She sees something I cannot. She stops communicating with me at this point. I wonder if she sees her parents and siblings. Her hand still holds tightly on to the rail and she is blue in color. The hospice nurse comes in to check on her. The nurse tries to move Clara's hand, but can't. I tell the nurse that Clara likes her hand there and not to try to move it. The nurse asks me about giving Clara morphine to help slow down her respiration and help with her passing. I tell her Clara had expressed she did not want medication. The nurse tells me that the previous week, Clara was okay with the morphine. I am skeptical. However, if Clara said it was fine, then I am okay with it, too.

It is 10:40 a.m. Clara is still holding on to the rail. Her hand is blue, and her eyes and mouth are open. She is still looking up at the ceiling. It almost seems that she is talking to someone, the way her mouth opens and closes.

While Clara is dying, I'm listening to another resident down the hall yell, "Help me! Help me!" over and over. In Clara's room, on the other side of the curtain, her roommate is having a discussion with her husband about a $10.00-off coupon for senior citizens, and another 50 percent off a coffeemaker at Kohl's. It's funny that they're talking about this while their neighbor on the other side of the curtain, the coupon queen, is dying. Maybe it's a sign—a tribute to Clara. They're also watching *The Price Is Right* on TV, so the sound of the beeping and spinning of games is in the background. Clara is dying and I'm listening to *The Price Is Right*. On the one hand, it seems inappropriate, given Clara's condition. But on the other hand, I can't help but think that having a show about pricing—especially grocery pricing—on the TV somehow honors Clara. I don't think Clara can hear any of it.

I smell terrible as I sit here, sweating. I stand up for a few minutes to stretch and throw out some apples and oranges that I had brought to Clara last week. They have fruit flies.

Clara is now making interesting movements with her mouth; a kind of square movement. When the beeping and spinning from *The Price Is Right* slows and stops, I think Clara is going to stop.

I quietly ask Clara what she's holding on for. I tell her that she needs to let go. She wouldn't like me sitting here wasting time. She would want me out, getting things done. I want to tell her to hurry up, so I can go. What a terrible thought this is. The nurse comes in and tells me that Clara had a bowel movement today. She says that the dying usually clear themselves out at the end. The nurse also says that Clara's feet aren't blue yet, like the feet of some others when they're dying. I think this may mean that Clara is not going quickly. But I can hardly see her breathing anymore. Just her mouth is moving, but only slightly.

I step out of the room to stretch my legs. I come back into the room and her chest is not moving up and down anymore—or it is moving so slightly that I can hardly see it. I don't want to get very close to her to check. Her mouth is still moving. Her roommate turns off the TV at 11:04 a.m. and leaves the room. It is peaceful and the sun shines in the window. There is a strange movement on the right side of her neck. Clara is taking her last breath.

11:11 a.m.

Clara passes away. No morphine. She dies before they ever get a chance to give it to her. She must have known. I stare at her for a little while—kind of in wonder, and taking in the fact that she's really gone. I keep looking at the clock.

I go into the hallway to let the nurses know that she has passed away. I say to them, "I think she passed away." And they say, "Really?" They seem to be shocked that it happened so quickly. They come in, check her, and listen to her heart. They confirm that she's dead and do just what I've seen done in the movies; they look at their watches, check the clock, and speak out loud, stating the time of death.

I think Clara wanted to pass away while I was with her.

It was our Wednesday.

I glance back at Clara one more time as I leave her room. I follow the nurse to her station. Sholom calls Clara's nephew to ask what they should do with her things, and to find out which funeral home they should contact. Knowing I am responsible for all of this, I let Lyle know that Clara asked me to be the personal representative of her estate. I'm not sure if Lyle is surprised by this or not. Either way, he knows the task ahead of me and is kind enough to spend some time on the phone giving me some direction. More important, being Clara's next of kin, Lyle gives permission for Sholom to allow me the ability to dictate what happens.

The nurse hands me Clara's worn-out blue purse and small blue overnight bag. It's the same bag that I grabbed for her three weeks ago today, the day I found her lying on her kitchen floor. I think Clara and I both knew that day that she would not return home.

It feels strange that she's gone and that I'm responsible for her things. Clara's watch and ring should still be in her wallet. It seems forever ago that I put them there when her hand was so thin and frail. I feel weird leaving with Clara's two blue bags. I remind myself that she asked me to do this. I call both Joy and Valerie to let them know that Clara passed away.

I walk out of Sholom, and I can feel the heavy burden that I have been carrying for the past eighteen months lift. I had a hard time saying no to Clara, and in some ways I am relieved that she finally passed away. I am now free from my constant worrying about her. However, my duty to Clara does not end with her death, and my moment of peace is quickly replaced by thoughts about her apartment. I want to run over there and start cleaning, to hurry up and get it all over with. This is how I am, and maybe that's why Clara asked me to do this. I am scared and grossed out thinking about what I will find.

I knew I had met Clara for a reason. Even from the very beginning, I knew our relationship was special. A year and a half ago, I wanted to be a volunteer. I thought I would simply go grocery shopping with an elderly person, maybe have nice conversations once a week. But it was evident from the beginning that Clara would be much more. Had I taken on more responsibility than I needed to? Clara needed me. Two similar people were brought together, her to be helped, and me . . . Maybe I was brought to Clara to see the similarities between us.

I'm not Clara, nor will I ever be, but had I met Clara in any other circumstance, I would have never known how special she really was. I would have known her as a smelly and cranky old woman. But who was she, really? Clara was a woman who worked hard and did things by the book. Her love of children and education led her to live a life of frugality so she could provide for others in her death. I have a big project ahead of me. I think Clara knew that, and I also think she knew I would do it her way. Larry said that it would take me four to six months to get everything sorted. I'm guessing it could take me more than a year. Clara would want me to take charge and just do it. That's what I'm going to do.

I have a million of my own things that I need to get done right now, too. I had set aside my life to take care of Clara. My daughter has a lacrosse game that I need to go to. I stop at home to put Clara's purse and bag away for safekeeping. But where am I going to keep a smelly, contaminated purse and bag? I'm afraid to keep them in my basement. I want them near me. Clara's keys, wallet, and safety deposit box key are in her purse. The purse will be my first clue about who Clara was, and it's where I need to start.

I decide to keep them in my bedroom. As gross as that is, they need to be where I can see them. Ted is at home, and we leave for the lacrosse game. We're driving when my cell phone rings. Ted answers it, since I'm driving, and he takes the call. It's from Tom, the director of the funeral home—or as Clara referred to it, "the Jewish morgue." Tom asks if Clara will be buried in a shroud. I don't realize it at the time, but this is the first of many questions that I need to answer for Clara. Tom explains, saying that it's a Jewish tradition that an individual be covered in a shroud. Clara was Jewish. I better do it.

Knowing that Tom would need to contact the cemetery, I tell him that Clara is to be buried in Superior, next to her sister. We set up a meeting for tomorrow to go over the details. It seems a bit odd that I'm planning the funeral and burial for a woman I had only known for a short period of time.

I'm too overwhelmed and lost in my thoughts to notice that my daughter's team wins the lacrosse game.

Even though I'm in a daze, I don't think Clara's death truly hits me until I start receiving calls that evening. *"We heard about Clara. We're so sorry."* Why are people calling me? And why do they say, "I'm sorry." Everyone thinks that because I spent so much time helping Clara, I cared deeply for her. The truth is, I felt an obligation toward Clara. I'm not sure if Clara ever really cared for me, either. She obviously trusted me. And I think it's right to say that we liked each other in our own ways.

I truly believe that our liking one another was mutual, even though at times it was obvious that Clara held back her frustrations with me. It wasn't that I did anything terribly wrong; it was just the way Clara was. She had no filter and seemed to be angry at everybody for something. However, with me, she seemed to hold it in; I don't think she was willing to risk losing her personal assistant and handyman.

One of Clara's cousins also calls to tell me that Clara died. It's funny, since I was the one who was with her when she died. I am up most of the night. So many things go through my mind. I'm scared because I'm not quite sure what's ahead of me. I'm happy to do this for Clara, although at the moment I'm tired.

Thursday, April 19, 2012

I arrive at the funeral home and am directed to a small sitting area where I wait for Tom. I sit for a moment and think of Clara. I picture Clara wrapped in a shroud. She's now a wax figure, similar to those in wax museums. I saw several of my family members after they died and I can still remember their waxen features. I can only assume Clara would take on the same after-death appearance.

Tom walks into the room and introduces himself. I follow him into a conference room and we begin to discuss plans for Clara. We first confirm her burial spot. Clara had told me before she died that she had a plot. I was glad to hear that it was paid for and ready to go. Knowing Clara, I'm not surprised by this.

I am very nervous about making any wrong decisions or giving Tom wrong information. I call Clara's nephew Lyle a couple times, just for reassurance. As Tom goes through the burial costs, I start to get anxious and begin to sweat. This is my first experience handling Clara's money. I need to be responsible. I can't believe how much burials cost. Sounding like Clara, I say to Tom, "It costs a lot of money to die."

He responds, "It sure does."

After I get over my anxiety about her burial costs, we go into another room to select a casket. I'm overwhelmed. There are so many to choose from. My choices range from a box that looks like something I could build in the garage to one extravagant enough for a queen.

I know that Clara didn't like to spend a lot of money, but how could I possibly put her in the cheapest selection? In many ways, my entire year and a half spent with Clara was like a comedy show. Why should today be any different? Looking for caskets for Clara is strange, funny, and very typical of our relationship. It kind of reminds me of our shopping. I want to call Clara to see which one I should pick.

I find a feminine, shapely casket with a Star of David on it. It is modest and one of the less expensive ones. I feel Clara would approve. It's the one I would select for myself. Clara and I are similar in certain ways, so I think this one is best.

We go back to the conference room and I give Tom the obituary Joy sent me. No survivors are included. Joy said this was the obituary that Clara wrote several years ago. Tom tells me that I can get a 10-percent discount if I pay in full right now. Clara liked discounts. I feel as if I should have a coupon for this! I call Larry, and he instructs me to wait to pay until I set up the estate account; then I'll pay from that. He suggests that I have the funeral home bill the estate. I see there are many things I will need to learn! I schedule Clara's funeral for 10:00 a.m.

the following morning. I set the day and time to fit my schedule.

After I leave the funeral home, I go to Clara's apartment and start to go through a few of her things. I begin with a pile of papers and find a letter from the JFCS responding to an inquiry Clara had made about bedbugs back during the fall of 2010. Oh no! I calculate in my mind when I started coming to her apartment. Yuck; she better not have bedbugs. What did I get into?

I have a hard time figuring out exactly where to start going through her things. I've never done anything like this before. I check a few more piles of paper and find there's a lot that I'll need to deal with. Her apartment is filthy and smells terrible. I throw away some more old food that I think may be the culprit, but I'm not sure I've really found the source of the bad smell. I open the screen door for a while to let some fresh air in. I get rid of some of her magazines and water her plants. I decide that I need to get through her funeral before I can focus on this place.

Friday, April 20, 2012

Margie happily offers to come with me to Superior
for Clara's funeral. I call and excuse her from school. I
drive the three hours while Margie talks and listens to
music from her iPod. Spending time with her in the car
brings back memories of all the college visits we took last
summer. I start to tear up, knowing that Margie will leave
for school in the fall. It also brings back memories of my
calls to Clara to check in with her during my travels.

Margie and I are at a gas station in Superior when my
phone rings. It's Joy. She's on her way to the funeral, but
just got a flat tire and won't make it in time. I wonder if
Clara has something to do with this. Joy is so kind and I
know she wants to be there for Clara. I feel bad that she
won't make it.

The cemetery is on the outskirts of the city. The location
is quite unique; it's not like the cemeteries we have in the
Cities. It is accessed by a very hilly dirt road. The setting
is farmlike and very beautiful. I spot Lyle, Clara's nephew,
as we pull into the cemetery. I recognize him from the

pictures I saw at Clara's. He is well dressed in a long black coat and a hat. He is very distinguished looking. I walk up to him and he grins, knowing who I am.

"Step into my office," he says to Margie and me. Lyle has a very good sense of humor. Before Clara died, she requested that he read the Mourner's Kaddish for her.

Lyle brought a cousin along with him. After Lyle and I speak for a bit, he calls a friend of his that he wants to come to the funeral. Five minutes later, Lyle's friend drives up the dirt road to join us. Margie and I crack up, because it's as if Lyle's friend has appeared out of thin air. We all walk over to Clara's burial spot. The five of us stand in a line, facing Clara's casket. Nearby are three individuals from the funeral home; they drove Clara up to Superior in a van. This, too, strikes me as kind of funny, because I picture dead people being driven around in hearses, not in cargo vans. I stare at the casket I selected set above the hole in the ground. I should be mourning; however, all I can think of is whether I selected the right one.

Lyle reads the Kaddish, just as Clara requested. I stand staring as Clara's casket is lowered into the ground. I only knew her for such a short time.

The five of us all perform the Jewish ritual of using the back of the shovel to put dirt into the grave. Clara is buried alongside her sister. Clara told me on Monday that she wanted a headstone like her parents'. I ask Lyle to take me to the plot where her parents are buried. He does, and I stare at the stone, trying to make a mental note of what it looks like. I walk back and take one last look at Clara beneath the ground, thinking of the strange, but special time we had. I say good-bye.

Clara died on Wednesday and was buried on Friday. It was how she would have liked it.

Part 2

The following section of this journal is a summary of my notes and thoughts during the time I spent taking care of Clara's estate.

Cleaning

It has been a difficult year, ending with the death of someone who tested me perhaps more than anyone else ever has. Yet, I feel a bond with Clara more than I have with anyone outside of my immediate family. In a way, I cared for her, and yet here I am, frustrated at what comes next. I'm responsible for cleaning up after her. All this time I've wanted Clara to take care of her stuff before she passed away and she did nothing—well, nothing except assign the cleanup to me.

I anticipate that settling Clara's estate is going to be more work than I originally thought. I'm starting to feel very anxious. From what I've read, my job as her personal representative is a big responsibility, and very time consuming. Clara's entire estate must go to the children's fund that is set up in her name. Where do I begin? The attorney told me to first set up an estate account. I will need to wait for her death certificate and my letter from the court stating that I'm Clara's personal representative before I can do anything, though.

It's been several days since Clara passed and I have yet to look in her purse. I have been too afraid. For some reason, I feel that going through her purse violates her trust in me, as if she is still alive and will get mad when she finds me looking at her things without her permission. I know this is silly. I know that she asked me to do this and that she's gone, but it's how I feel.

I sit down on my bedroom floor and open her old, worn-out, blue purse. I feel like I'm being sneaky. I remind myself again that she asked me to do this. I take out her wallet. Surprise! It's blue. I had seen her wallet before, but never really paid attention to the color until now. I count her cash, review her credit cards, and, more importantly, find the safety deposit box key that she said would be here. I know which bank holds her box because I remembered to ask her a few days before she died if she had one, and where I would find the key. I also find her blue coupon pocketbook holder in her purse. I had seen this on most of our shopping escapades. It's filled with coupons. They're alphabetized from A to Z. I leave the coupons in the purse for now. Clara would not be happy if I threw coupons away.

I'm on my first official day of cleanup and I'm prepared with paper towels and soap. Upon walking into Clara's apartment, I can smell the nastiness; it's disgusting. I know where I'll start. I walk to the cabinets in the kitchen and open them all. They're filled with the cans of peaches, vegetables, and other fruits she insisted on buying every week. These are the same cans I complained she wasn't eating. Yet I let her buy them, afraid to tell her no.

I go to the basement of her building and get the red grocery cart that I had used several weeks ago to bring her trash and recycling to the garage. I load the cans that are not expired into the cart. I wheel the cart to my car and load them in. I drive over to a local organization that helps people in emergency situations and donate them. There are 115 pounds of canned goods. The organization is happy to receive such a large donation. Driving away, I can't help but wonder if this was the plan Clara had in mind all along.

Clara's apartment is so dusty and dirty that I need to find someone else to clean it. Sue had been referred to me because of her excellent cleaning and organizational skills. Sue is amazing. She spends several days during my first few weeks at the apartment cleaning things I will not touch: toilets, shower, bathtub, kitchen cabinets, and the area behind the refrigerator and stove. She recommends cleaning supplies that might help remove the cemented-on stains in the toilets, tub, and shower. Unfortunately, nothing works on the stains.

Sue kindly listens to me for weeks as I sort through Clara's stuff. I keep interrupting her cleaning to show her interesting things that I find. She offers advice and wisdom about what to do in the apartment, including what to do with Clara's stuff. The problem for both Sue and me is that the more things I pull out of cabinets, drawers, and closets, the more the dust grows. We both quickly realize that Clara did not throw anything away!

Sorting

Clara has kept every piece of clothing she's ever owned
dating back to the 1940s, perhaps even the 1930s,
including bras (I have never seen bras like this before!),
shoes, hats, stockings, and scarves. Three closets have
clothes piled from top to bottom. Clara has every shoe
she ever wore. Once she was done wearing the pair, it
apparently went right back into the box, never to be
thrown out, but rather stacked high to the ceiling. Most
of the shoes look too worn to sell or even donate. She
also kept every purse and wallet she ever used. She kept
all sets of suitcases dating back to the '30s, cramming them
in her closet. The quality of some of her things is amazing.

Clara told me that she worked in women's retail
as a buyer. She really knew how to buy! She has large
quantities of shirts, pants, dresses, and pantsuits. I fill her
entire living room with bags stuffed full of her clothes. I
have a problem, though, and laugh to myself thinking that
Clara would have also called it a problem: the front closet
has three mink-fur coats and one beaver-fur coat. One
of the mink coats and the beaver coat are falling apart

because moths have eaten them. What a shame. I have to toss them. A wonderful light-colored mink shawl and a gorgeous long, brown mink have been spared. I'll be able to sell these!

Clara's blue coat, with her blue gloves that she wore during our shopping days stuffed into the pockets, is still in the closet; it's covered with her wiry white hair and dandruff. I'm not yet ready to let it go. I leave it hanging in the closet. Sitting on the shelf above her blue coat are two pairs of rubber boots, still in their boxes. These are identical to the boots I duct taped for her last year. Had I known she had two brand new, unopened boxes of them in the closet, I would have made her take them out and use them. I also find several sets of sheets and blankets, and yet Clara slept on a sheet and blanketless bed. Why did she not put these on her bed? I really wonder if she actually knew what she had here.

The cans of food are gone and the clothes are bagged up. I've thrown out so much, and yet the apartment seems almost worse than before I started. I still have months to go. I can't believe how much stuff she has. I find tax returns dating back to the '50s, receipts, daily calendars dating back to the '60s, letters, notebooks, pens, lists, pencils, old check stubs, vintage school supplies, old keys, cases of tinfoil, cases of paper plates, cases of plastic silverware, unopened boxes of pots and pans, toys, shelves of books, broken sink parts, old carpet, multiple can openers, several toasters, Barbie items, baseball memorabilia, free stuff from cereals boxes, free mail giveaways, two typewriters, phones, three televisions (two of which are old and don't work), several cases of Pledge, many empty and dusty boxes, and piles of other broken junk.

This stuff is only a fraction of what she has crammed into her closets. Why would she keep some of this stuff? So much of it is broken. I'm upset and frustrated with her. I thought she was frugal, but isn't this beyond frugal? A lot of it is the free, giveaway stuff that she probably sent away for or received as a gift when she ordered something. Much of the stuff never even made it out of boxes, either.

Every shelf, cabinet, bookcase, and drawer is packed with things. Even her buffet is jammed full of stuff. Hers is only a two-bedroom apartment; how could she have kept the amount of stuff in here that she did?

Clara did not use cups, only jars. I remember this from when I unloaded her dishwasher a couple of months ago. She has several kitchen cabinets filled with them. They look like mayonnaise jars. I'll recycle these. I find several sets of drinking glasses in her dining room china cabinet. Why didn't she use these instead?

I just don't have time to be doing this. I'm mad at Clara for putting me in this position.

I start to separate items into piles: garbage, recycle, donate, and sell. It's difficult to make room for additional piles, because her entire apartment is already filled with furniture and regular household items you would find in any home. I am pressed for space when piling.

I go through Clara's things every day, trying to sort out the mess. I need to rely on her mail and her very large pile of papers to find out more about her finances. While I want to throw some stuff away, I also get a nauseated feeling thinking that I may be tossing something of importance. I keep thinking that this process is going to get better, but it doesn't. The apartment continues to smell and I still cannot figure out why. When it's time to sell (it's a condominium, actually, not an apartment, as Clara always called it), I fear that I won't find someone who wants to live here. Even empty, it still may be smelly. I need to get this place ready to sell.

Clara gets more junk mail then I've ever seen. On most of it I write, "Deceased; return to sender," then put it back into the outgoing mail. All other correspondence I keep, knowing I will need it to settle her estate.

About two weeks after Clara's death, I receive the important documentation that I need to begin working on the financial part of her estate. I wonder if all those times Clara told me that she had too much money in her checking—looking to me for a reaction—she was actually testing me about whether or not she could trust me to take care of her money after she was gone. I really wonder at what point she started thinking about all of this. All those times that she would stare at me with that Clara look; was she considering it? Why did she wait until the end? She was smart and knew that I had a hard time saying no to her. Maybe she chose to ask me at a very vulnerable time, knowing I would not turn her down.

I set up an estate account at one bank, and then go to the bank where her safety deposit box is. I'm very anxious as I present all the appropriate paperwork to the banker so I can have access to her box. This feels weird—me going into Clara's safety deposit box. It takes the banker a while to verify the documents before I'm allowed into the vault. Although I'm nervous, I'm also excited to see what's in the box. With Clara, you just never know.

I find several items relating to her finances. She also has the kind of unusual things that I have come to expect from Clara: thirty-three silver dollars, state quarters, stamps, and other miscellaneous items that she must have thought were of value. I leave everything in the box, except for the financial information that I need.

I bring the financial papers to my house and put them in Clara's blue travel bag that I have next to her purse. I never noticed this before, but the bag has the name *Time* on it. It must have been a free gift from *Time* magazine, sent to her for ordering a subscription.

The next few weeks are much of the same thing. I spend half of my time sorting out her finances, which takes an immense amount of work. Consulting with the accountant and attorney, and meeting with the representatives at each financial institution is a job in itself.

The other half of my time I spend cleaning out her apartment to get it ready for sale. The dust, dirt, and filth seem never-ending, and are intolerable. I have become frustrated and angry about everything. The stress is really getting to me. I want to cry, and I do! I try not to complain to anyone about how I'm feeling. If I do, I hear the same thing: "You should have never said yes to her." I know I brought this on myself. I don't need others to remind me.

This is strange; I act like Clara when I'm in her apartment. It's almost as if she's directing me. Taking care of Clara's estate is like a daily episode of a comedy show. What could go wrong, does go wrong.

Mail

About two to three weeks after Clara dies, her mail starts to taper off. This strikes me as a bit odd. Each day, there's less and less mail, and eventually there's no mail. I become concerned. Where is Clara's mail going?

I stop by her local post office to inquire. I carry my PR letter and Clara's death certificate everywhere with me now. I need these at all times. No one will talk to me without them. I meet with the manager at the post office and she assures me that no one has turned in any forwarding notices for Clara's mail, and that all the mail is getting delivered properly to her box. I'm not convinced, but I accept what she says.

For days, Clara still gets no mail. I know something is wrong. I happen to be in the lobby of her building when I see the caretaker. I ask him if he knows anything about Clara's mail. He says he'll ask the postal carrier. He later finds me and tells me the story. As it turns out, on one of the days I wrote "Deceased; return to sender" on some junk mail, a new substitute postal carrier had started delivering the mail. He took it upon himself to return all of Clara's mail that day, and on all the days after.

Oh no! A month of missing mail. This is a huge problem! I rely on Clara's mail to figure out almost everything. Losing a month of mail is disastrous, because I have no idea what I'm even missing. I'm sure that many important documents had been returned to the sender, including bills, checks, and both Social Security and retirement information. The carrier has no idea of the severity of the problem he's caused. I'm furious. I don't need this added stress.

I go back to the post office to complain. The manager apologizes and says the carrier is not allowed to return or forward the mail without written permission from me. The damage is done. More complaining will not do me any good. If this had happened to Clara, she would have yelled at them. However, I'm not good with confrontation. I let it go, and just deal with the setback as best I can.

It takes a tremendous amount of time to figure out all that's missing and replace or correct things.

Shredding

Clara's desk in her den is packed with more stuff than I've ever seen. I'm frustrated because I have to go through every single piece of paper to figure out if I need it or not. I have to be very careful not to throw away anything that I may need in order to settle her estate. This is a difficult task. Every time I open up a new drawer or cabinet, I find more and more. At first I found this interesting. Now I'm getting angry, discouraged, and continually disgusted by the dirtiness of it all. This is a nightmare!

Clara literally has kept every financial document that she could. Most of it cannot be recycled or tossed because of the private information on it. It needs to be shredded. I have to bring it all to my house and use my shredder. I spend several days shredding Clara's financial statements, blank checks, old cashed checks, invoices, tax returns, and receipts (all dating back to the '50s), just to name a few. All the shredding takes a toll on my shredder, which breaks midway through. I spend the next few days tearing the papers by hand. I am not happy!

I overstuff my own recycling bin several times and put extra bags out alongside it. I get a note taped to my bin from the recycling carrier saying that I'm only allowed to put out what fits in the bin with the top closed.

Jewelry

I find Clara's jewelry in an old, musty jewelry box in her dresser drawer. The jewelry looks antique and is very interesting. I'm not sure if it's of any value, though, because much of it looks like costume jewelry. However, the stuff is cool—very vintage. I find some more state quarters in the drawer, too. I'll need to deposit these.

I spend a lot of time on my computer, researching many of Clara's personal items. I want to make sure I have an idea of what some of the items are worth. If something is of great value, I need to know. I also have several estate-sale companies look at Clara's things to help me figure out what to do with it all. Every company tells me the same thing: her stuff is not worth moving to a different location for a sale. Apparently, it's mostly garage-sale stuff. The building manager tells me that I'm not allowed to have a sale that's open to the public in the building.

   The estate-sale people recommend that I just try to sell things to some of the local antique dealers or have a sale for just the residents in Clara's building. My neighbor,

Jan, who has listened to me talk about Clara for over a year, is interested in looking at Clara's jewelry to see if there's something she wants to buy. I have brought several of Clara's items to my house: jewelry, coins, etc. I am afraid that, since no one is living in her apartment, someone might go in and take her things. I feel it's best to keep the stuff with me. The problem is, the stuff is musty and stinks like an old person's home. Yuck.

Jan comes over and looks at the jewelry. She picks out some pieces that she's interested in. I can't sell the items to her yet because of the thirty-day probate waiting period. I set the pieces aside for her.

Jan tells me about a small vintage jewelry shop nearby. I take Clara's jewelry there. The owner values it and gives me a price for all the items she'd like to purchase. She also gives me an idea about what I should charge Jan for the items that she's interested in. Because my thirty-day waiting period is not up yet, I leave with Clara's jewelry.

Joy

I speak with Joy often, and we exchange Clara stories.
She tells me that she met Clara at a family gathering and
somehow their relationship developed into her helping
Clara for many years. Joy did the same kind of shopping
with Clara that I had most recently done. Clara knew a
lot about Joy, and spoke of her to me. I thought Clara just
knew Joy because she was a distant cousin who would
help out periodically. I was surprised to hear that Joy did a
lot for Clara for many years.

Joy has been offering to help me. She feels terrible that
I was left to clean up after Clara. However, I reassure her
that it's okay, reminding her I agreed to it. I like talking
with Joy. It's another person to run things by. However,
at times I feel as if Clara is breathing down my neck or
looking over my shoulder, telling me not to talk about
her things or allow anyone into her apartment.

I take Joy up on her offer to help, and ask her to meet
me at Clara's on a Saturday. I have an appointment with
an antique dealer, and I feel I could use Joy's support.
Saturday is a gloomy day, and I'm not in the mood to

spend a long time at Clara's. It's dark and uncomfortable in her apartment, and her things are all over the tables, chairs, and floor. After over an hour looking through Clara's things, the dealer asks me if Clara has any sterling. I've been keeping the sterling in a cabinet and had not yet brought it to my house for safekeeping with the other items. My gut is telling me not to take out the sterling.

Joy and I look at each other. I know I have to start selling Clara's things. The thirty-day waiting period is now up. I reluctantly take out the sterling. The dealer looks it over and gives me a price. I have not gotten it appraised yet. However, I remember what my mom sold her sterling for, so I have a general idea about the proper price range. The dealer and I start to negotiate.

During the negotiations, there's a lightning bolt and a very loud crack of thunder, the kind that makes you jump and plug your ears. Clara must be telling me that the price we're negotiating is too low. With a pit in my stomach, I sell the sterling. I don't feel good about this. I can't figure out if this is because I feel the price is too low, or I'm afraid of letting go of Clara's things. I take photos of everything I sell, including the sterling, and the dealer leaves.

Something doesn't seem right. Clara is telling me something. The price is too low. I express my concerns to Joy. She assures me that it's okay, and that I need to let things go and not to worry so much. For me, this is terribly hard to do!

I can't let it go. I'm making myself sick over the fact that I sold the sterling for too low a price; I think I could get more. The dealer had told me when she was leaving Clara's that she was going to work at the antique shop. I want Clara's sterling silver back and I need to talk to the dealer. I close up the apartment and go to the antique shop and tell the dealer that I want the sterling back. The dealer is anxious and tells me she can't talk with me about it while she's working.

I feel terrible that I'm bothering her at work. She's such a nice lady. Why am I doing this to her? We set a date of Tuesday at noon for her to meet me at Clara's, and she agrees to bring back the sterling. She's not happy with me. I'm not happy with myself, either! I leave and go to the vintage jewelry shop that I had been to before. I sell Clara's jewelry, some silver dollars, and a gold coin. I hope that whomever buys the jewelry from the shop knows how special it is. I'm sad to let go of Clara's watch and ring. I have to keep reminding myself she told me to sell everything.

Larry asked Clara a few times during the preparation and signing of her will if she wanted any of her personal belongings to go to anyone. Each time he asked, Clara would shake her head and say no. I was hoping that she would want to give her watch and ring to someone in her family. I really struggle with this issue. At times, I want to give her belongings to relatives. People keep telling me that I am her PR and can decide what to do with her things. I keep coming back to the fact that Clara said it should all be sold. I'm doing what Clara said to do.

I spend some time counting the coins that I find in her safety deposit box and in her bedroom dresser drawers. I go to the bank to make a deposit. The bank will not take the silver dollars. What? Isn't a bank supposed to take money? They say they have no use for them. I leave and go to another bank. This bank cashes them for dollars and tells me they often have requests from their customers for silver dollars. I go back to the other bank and make the deposit.

Several people ask me if I'm going to keep something of Clara's to remember her by. I had only known Clara for a year and a half. Clara said, "Sell everything." That's what Clara said, so that's what I'm doing. I know that if Clara wanted me to have something, she would have told me.

The clutter at Clara's continues to be overwhelming and I continue to be very anxious. Every few days I make several trips with the red cart up and down the elevator to the large garbage and recycling dumpsters in the garage of Clara's building. I try to be considerate of the other residents in the building and not monopolize the dumpsters. It's very hard, though. I completely fill the dumpsters five or six times. This is not stuff to be sold. This is actual garbage and papers.

It's insane. Being a germ freak, I'm having a hard time dealing with all these garbage runs. I sweat terribly because the cart is very heavy with all the junk in it. The more I can get in the cart at one time, the fewer amount of times I have to go up and down the elevator. Dragging all the stuff from her unit down the hall and to the elevator is cumbersome. Each time I go in the elevator, I pack it full. No one can get in and ride down. My hands are raw, cut up, and constantly bleeding from all my hand washing.

Why am I doing this? I won't pay anyone to do this work, though, because Clara would be upset if I spent the money on that, when I can do it all myself. I think this is another thing she saw in me.

The antique dealer brings back the sterling and purchases some other items from Clara's estate. I don't think she's happy about bringing back the sterling; however, she is very understanding and empathic to my situation. I thank her. After she leaves, another dealer I have scheduled comes over and buys the shoulder fur that was untouched by the moths, as well as some other items. She also pays me more for the sterling, $300.00 more than I was first offered. I had checked on the value, so I knew how much I could get for it. This dealer has also brought her brother. He buys an old phone, some postcards, a couple of ceramic bowls, a poster, and some other miscellaneous items.

They leave and I unbag all ten bags of clothing to have accessible for a clothing dealer to view. A woman from a vintage clothing store I've contacted comes by and looks through Clara's clothes. She sits down on the floor next to all of the clothes and begins talking, saying that she's having a really hard day, and proceeds to tell me all about it. I'm like a magnet for people with problems. I kindly listen to her as she looks through Clara's things. She only purchases a few items: one pantsuit, one blazer, three dresses, a couple of slips, one nightgown, a purse, a hat, and an umbrella. That's it.

I'm shocked. I thought someone would want the entire collection. Am I missing something? The clothing dealer shows me that more than half of Clara's things are stained. I didn't notice this before. I'm stuck with ten bags of clothes that I should just donate. However, I can't get myself to do this yet. I need to try to sell the clothes first. There has to be another place out there that will buy all of this.

I contact another vintage clothing store a couple weeks later and make arrangements to meet the owner of the store at Clara's. I go to Clara's and again unbag the ten bags. The dealer is a very nice woman, but like the previous dealer, she only buys a couple of items. I ask her the same question I asked before, why no one wants to buy Clara's clothes. She tells me that all of Clara's clothing and accessories are too matronly. Now I understand— stained and matronly. Of course no one wants the stuff. I bag up all the clothes again. Everyone tells me to just get rid of everything. "Toss it or donate it," they say. I'm trying to do what Clara asked.

Each time I sell something, I immediately go to the bank to make the deposit. The bank tellers look at me funny when I make deposits of $2.00, $5.00, $8.00, twenty-five quarters, etc. I have this fear that if I keep Clara's cash in my purse from the things I sell, I will accidentally spend it and forget what is hers and what is mine. I feel like Clara is looking over my shoulder. I cannot mix our money. My anxieties take me right to the bank and make the deposit, regardless of how small it is. This is another Clara attribute that I have!

Sale

Clara's building caretaker stops by often to see how things are going. I speak with him regarding the sale that I'm planning. Maybe I can get rid of some of her things by selling them to people in her building. But I need to get the approval from the board to have a sale for the residents.

A week before the sale, I post flyers on each floor and in the lobby of her building. I'm curious to see if any of the residents will actually come by. I spend all Friday at Clara's pricing everything in her apartment. I have a feeling that this is not going to be a successful sale. However, I feel that I have to try.

Saturday, I have the sale, and my stepfather spends the day helping me. Approximately ten residents stop by. I also tell my friend Lea about the sale. She is kind enough to come by with her sister and buy some of Clara's things. I meet some really nice residents from Clara's building. My favorite is a young woman who has recently moved into the building. She is looking for things to fill her own apartment. She notices the funny-looking antenna that I gave to Clara last winter. I've been so busy with everything that I forgot the antenna is still here, connected to Clara's TV. The young woman asks if the antenna works. I tell her it does and give it to her so she can try it out in her apartment.

I sell a fraction of Clara's items and make a total of $80.00. This was not a good use of my time. Clara would probably think otherwise. To Clara, $80.00 would have been a lot.

As I'm cleaning up and getting ready to leave, the young woman stops by to let me know that the antenna works great! I guess it was worth it to sit at Clara's the whole day just to give away my antenna and make someone happy. I even think Clara would be happy that someone's TV is now working.

I drive a carload of Clara books to a special vintage bookstore that I find during my research. Some of Clara's books look old and possibly collectible. I have to park a few blocks away from the store because there is no nearby parking. I have ten bags of books in my truck. It takes several trips back and forth to carry the books to the shop. An employee finally stops me and suggests that she goes to my car and have a look, rather than me dragging in the rest of the bags. The bookstore does not take one book. I take all the books back to Clara's.

It's time to donate whatever I can and have a garage sale for the more expensive items. Clara has china, antique tea sets, framed pictures, lamps, etc. that I still would like to try to sell. I spend several days packing up the items for donation. I make two full truckload deliveries of housewares to a place not far from Clara's. It's a volunteer organization that helps families get back on their feet after a crisis or during a transition. Everything that is donated to this organization goes to help families set up living spaces. Nothing is ever sold to these families, only given to them. I like this idea. The items they don't take I drive to another location for donating.

Sue's husband helps me by hauling away the three televisions from Clara's apartment. Sue loads her car with the ten bags of clothes (less the couple items I sold) and delivers them for me to another organization that helps people in emergencies. After she takes the bags to the donation place, she comes back and we load her entire truck with more items for donation to Goodwill.

Clara's apartment is still filled with things. However, it now looks like a regular home.

Carpet

It's time to get the carpets cleaned. They are terribly stained. A large stain sits in front of Clara's blue-and-white-striped chair. I remember in January when she got mad at me about the TV, choked on her Total cereal, and spit up on her carpet in front of the chair. The stain is still here. Sue has tried using her electric rug cleaner, but the carpet is so bad that Sue's cleaner can't get out any of the stains. I decide it's time to call a professional.

I call the carpet-cleaning service that I use for my own home. The same guy who has been cleaning my carpets for ten years shows up. Several years ago when he was cleaning my carpets, we got to talking about the chemicals that go into carpet cleaning. I'm neurotic about the toxicity of chemicals. A few years ago, I expressed my concerns to him. He laughed and told me that he lives in an apartment above a chemical company and doesn't worry about it. So now when I see him, I always ask him how it's going, living above the chemical company. I don't want him to get sick, and I worry about him—just like I do about everyone else.

A year ago when he came to my house, I was in the "bedbug" worry phase. He had just come from cleaning the rugs at a local restaurant. I was worried that he had brought "bedbugs" to my house. I hate the fact that I worry about everything all the time. It gets tiring. Clara never had bedbugs. The letter I found the first day of my cleaning adventures turned out to be nothing other than the fact that Clara had a rash, and someone suggested she check for bedbugs. Joy confirmed this for me.

The carpet is cleaned and deodorized. I stay away for a couple days to let it dry. I work on her finances and the documents for selling her condo. The time it takes me to transfer her assets goes way beyond what I expected. Working with the financial institutions, filling out forms, and getting special authorizations has really pushed me to the limit. I have to redo several transfers and make countless trips to the banks and post office. Things are very complicated and I try to stay calm, which is difficult right now. I am tense and I feel like my head is going to explode.

Clara's closets are for the most part clear, and the space doesn't look stuffed anymore. It just looks like a normal lived-in apartment—not like a hoarding situation, as it did before. My frustration is also starting to lessen, and I'm beginning to feel a bit more relaxed. I feel as if I'm through with the worst of it. I'm not sure which has been worse, though, sorting through her clutter or sorting through her finances. I meet with the city building inspector a couple of times to get her apartment up to code. I have a handyman neighbor of mine do all the work for the code compliance.

For the first few days or so after the carpets are cleaned it seems that the cleaning does the trick; the horrible smell seem to have vanished. However, it's starting to come back. It's amazing; the place still smells after a carpet cleaning! I'm not happy about this. The walls and furniture have probably absorbed the smell. The deodorizer that the carpet cleaner put on was just masking it. I need to find something that will get rid of the smell.

I purchase a spray-on deodorizer from the store and give the carpets a good spraying. This seems to help a bit.

Rummage

I still have the china, pictures, antique tea sets, collectibles, and other small items to sell. I convince my sister to have a garage sale at her house. It's a better location for traffic than my own home. I pack my truck full with Clara's things and spend all day Friday setting up. I arrive early Saturday morning at my sister's and drag the tables and sale items into the driveway. After a full day of haggling and negotiating with shoppers about Clara's stuff, the estate makes $130.00. Take away the cost of advertising and the net is $85.00. It wasn't worth the time!

I load my truck with all the items that didn't sell and drive them back to Clara's. While it didn't make much money, the garage sale did make a good thing happen: I met Don. He helps underprivileged adults set up housing. At the sale of Clara's items at my sister's, Don was looking for beds and dressers, which I did not have. However, I have Clara's bed at her apartment and I need to get rid of it. We set a time to meet at Clara's the following day for him to take the bed.

Don shows up on time with his wife to help, and they happily take Clara's bed. He tells me that her furniture is too nice to take. I then tell him I have a dresser at my house that he can have, too. It is my husband's from when he was a child. Don follows me to my house and takes the dresser. I am happy to help Don. He is doing a good thing helping people.

The time has come for me to donate the rest of Clara's personal belongings. Maybe I should have just donated everything from the start, like everyone suggested.

I decide to give the apartment another deodorizing. I've used up my first bottle of deodorizer. I will try my next purchase: a powder pour on. I sprinkle the eliminator on the carpet. Wow; that's potent! I instantly regret doing this, because there's a showing tonight at seven o'clock. What a turnoff the smell is. Yuck.

I have an allergic reaction, as I always do from these kinds of things. My head is pounding; I have to sit out on the balcony while the place airs out. I'm having a difficult time breathing, and I'm feeling sick, nauseated, and dizzy. I decide to leave for a while, but keep the sliding doors open to help get some of the potent smell out.

Two hours later, I'm back. The strong smell has subsided a bit. I want the apartment to look good for the showing tonight. I've had it on the market for a few weeks now. I haven't been getting good feedback from the showings. Upon entering, everyone says, "What's that smell?" No one is interested because of the smell. Also, no one likes the view of the power lines from the balcony—

there's a huge power line post right outside and it seems that all the power lines from the neighborhood go out from that particular post. People think it's a bad view.

I get an offer on Clara's condominium! I can't believe it. The woman loves the place, smell, power poles, and all. They always say in the real estate business that all it takes is the right buyer. I guess this woman is the one.

Today Clara's furniture and anything left over that I wasn't able to sell will be removed and donated to the Hope Chest. After several months of research, I selected the Hope Chest because of its mission, and the fact that they were willing to pick up and take everything that was left of Clara's. I get to Clara's about fifteen minutes before the movers. I quickly take pictures of all remaining items that will be picked up and donated today. I need these for the estate tax records. This is a bit of a challenge, because I have to unbox everything, take the photos, and then re-box it before the movers get here. I've never been so tired of looking at boxes!

During my re-boxing frenzy, a gentleman I've never met before stops by to see how things are going. He's someone associated with the building. Like everyone else I've met who knew Clara, he has something to say. They always try to say it nicely. He says something along the lines of, "Clara had her good days and bad days." I wonder if this is the gentleman who Clara called a liar a year ago. I smile, thank him for stopping by, and continue with my packing.

The Hope Chest movers arrive at 1:00 p.m. on the dot. Within two hours, all of Clara furniture, housewares, and pictures that I couldn't sell are gone. I don't let them take Clara's blue-and-white-striped chair, though. I heard that the new buyer likes the chair. I'm leaving it for her because I don't have it in my heart to remove it from Clara's apartment. Clara would be happy that it's staying. Clara's place actually looks pretty good. It's different than I expected.

Fur

I still have a few select items that I need to remove
from Clara's apartment: her blue jacket, a mink coat, a
collection of matchbooks, two boxes of vintage crayons,
photos, coins, stamps, and other miscellaneous personal
items. Clara had several hundred matchbooks that she
collected dating back to the 1930s. She must have picked
up a matchbook from every hotel, restaurant, and place
she ever visited. Many are from her travels around the
world. None of the antique dealers that visited her
apartment wanted them, and no one at any of the sales
seemed interested, either. I have kept them in the closet
of her den for several months. I've known they were
there; I just didn't have time to deal with them.

I can't throw that many matchbooks in the garbage—
too combustible. I just don't know what to do with them,
but they have to go. Every time I open up the closet, I get
nauseated; the sulfur smell from the matches is horrible.
When I sort and clean in the room with the matchbooks,
I get a headache, although it's the one room in her

apartment that hasn't had that other strange stale-food smell. But I can't stand the sulfur smell anymore.

On my way out, I grab the matchbooks, mink coat, crayons, stamps, and coins. I decide to spend the afternoon at a few other dealers that I haven't visited before. The smell of the matchbooks in my car gives me a pounding headache. If I don't sell them to anyone in an antique shop today, I will bring them to the fire station and let them dispose of them.

One of the dealers actually buys the bag of matches for $2.00—what a bargain. Next I sell the two sets of vintage crayons. The dealer pays me $6.00 for the two boxes. She's a teacher and thinks it will be fun to share the vintage crayons with her students. I go to another dealer across town that specializes in stamps and coins. I sell Clara's stamps and coins for $5.84. I wonder if Clara saved these things thinking they would be of value.

I don't have time to deal with her mink today, so I take it out of my car and hang it in the front hall closet of my house. It's in a garment bag. I have an uneasy feeling about the coat. I am carrying around a beautiful—yet kind of creepy—old mink coat from a woman who has died. I can't even imagine Clara ever wearing a coat like this.

The next day, I grab the coat and plan to visit a resale shop. However, I get too busy and the coat sits in my car for a few days. As usual, I obsess over it being in the back of my truck. I finally have time and stop at the resale shop with the coat in the garment bag.

The owner of the shop, who I had sold some of Clara's things to before, is working. She opens up the garment bag and fur flies everywhere. It gets in my mouth! My anxiety starts to mount.

It's the moths! They had gotten to this coat, too. I hadn't noticed this before. I am now worried with the fur flying everywhere that I must be getting it on my clothes. And more importantly, the fur coat had been in the closet of my house and in my car for a few days. I'm extremely upset.

The owner and I step outside while she bangs the coat around a bit more. The fur falls off in chunks. I step back; I really want to run down the block to get away from what's coming off the coat. The owner takes the coat back inside and makes some phone calls regarding the fur that's falling off. The owner gets confirmation from a specialist that the fur is worthless. What a waste!

Photos

Slowly, I've begun to piece together who Clara was. Sometimes I wonder if I became too close to her, too late in life. I knew her when she was a strong but bitter woman who had tossed everyone out of her life. She only allowed a limited few to be near her at the end. I suspect she cared for many people, despite being upset with them.

The last of Clara personal belongings I have stored in her den closet. I spend a lot of time in Clara's den, sitting on the floor, looking at her pictures. I'm sad as I look through her photos and letters, picturing a younger Clara who had the strength to travel the world. She had no kids of her own, and at the same time, she had hundreds. This is evident in the dozens of thank-you letters and volunteer service awards from the school district where she volunteered so much of her time.

I spend a good portion of my time looking through and deciding what to do with all her photos. I have met or spoken with several of Clara's relatives. Now, Joy and another cousin come to the apartment to look at the photos to help identify family members. While we are looking at the photos, her cousin gets very excited when he sees a photo he had given to Clara many years back. Apparently, Clara wanted to make a copy of this particular photo for herself. Her cousin never got the original back and kept pressing Clara for it. Clara insisted that she had returned it. They disagreed about who had it for years.

Knowing Clara, I can only image how these discussions went. Her cousin said that the disagreement over the photo put a strain on their relationship, and that Clara stopped talking to him. I give him back the photo. While we're looking through the family photos, he also tells me that education was very important to Clara's parents and to Clara. Her family made a big deal about being educated. He said that Clara would not even acknowledge people who were uneducated.

I could definitely see this in Clara. The year and a half we were together, Clara always talked about education. Each shopping day, she would ask me if Margie had selected a college yet. She would always let me know her opinion on college. I'm not surprised to hear her cousin reiterate what I had already thought about Clara and the importance she put on education.

Her cousins also help me identify different family members and figure out whom to send some of the other pictures to. After our meeting, I'm able to ship several boxes of Clara's photos to different family members.

During my time looking at Clara's photos, I also find the baby picture that Clara had said was Bob Dylan. There are a few other photos of him, too. Clara had saved several articles, newspaper clippings, posters, and memorabilia published on Bob Dylan. I return the personal photos of Dylan to his family and donate all the memorabilia and articles to the Hibbing Library for their Dylan collection.

And then there's Clara's photos of tennis player John McEnroe. Clara loved tennis. I remember her wanting to get home to watch Wimbledon on one of our shopping days. I find two photos of John McEnroe—one is signed. This must be the autograph that Clara told me she had gotten when she ran into him at Donaldson's years ago. From the way the photo looks, he was there signing pictures, not just shopping, as I had pictured when Clara told me the story. The photos are of McEnroe holding up a Wimbledon Cup, most likely from the '70s. The back of the photo says "To Clara" and it's signed "John McEnroe."

Clara corresponded with more than just relatives. She had friends all over the world. She has letters dating back to the early '30s. She was pen pals with many. One could have a world history lesson just from reading her letters.

I have read so many cards and thank-you notes to Clara—she kept them all. Clara was very giving to people. She sent baby gifts, shower gifts, birthday gifts, bar and bat mitzvah gifts, cards, and the list goes on. So many people sent Clara holiday cards, birthday cards, and letters, too. She corresponded with many. She also spent a good amount of time with relatives many years ago. This is something that she didn't do in her most recent years. Reading her letters gives me the feeling that at one point she was very close to them. I really wish I had known her years before.

Joy has been so helpful to me, and I'm grateful that she has been here to give me direction in certain areas. She has a kind heart and cared for Clara on many levels. Reading all the cards that she sent to Clara, I know that she and Clara were very close at one time. I feel sad that Clara pulled away from her, too. I give back to Joy all the cards that Clara saved from her.

Clara has also left the story of her life. She has yearbooks from her high-school days in Nashwauk, her junior college in Hibbing, and college at the University of Minnesota. She has her varsity letter awards, college transcripts, and career information—so much about her life! Most important for me, though, is that she kept her daily calendars dating back several decades. She used these calendars as a type of journal or diary. I'm learning so much about her just by reading her calendars. She would write about being sick and staying home from work. She wrote about disagreements with friends. In one of the entries, she describes arguing with a very good friend. Clara actually wrote what she said to her friend, and what the friend's response to Clara's comment was.

She wrote on days she visited family: what family members were doing, who was there, and how people were feeling. She wrote about her shopping, and all of her volunteer time at the school district. She wrote the names of the students she played checkers with, and who won the games! It was very evident that she cared for children and wanted to see that they were educated. Her volunteer time consisted of playing checkers, reading books, going on field trips, and assisting in the class wherever she was needed.

I also find every complaint letter and postcard she ever wrote. She wrote many, and when she did, she would keep a copy. When she received a response back regarding the complaint, she would re-respond in writing (keeping a copy, of course). Clara was very involved in politics, too. Several of her photographs show her attending different political events. She would write congresspeople. She even sent a sympathy card to Jackie Kennedy after President Kennedy died. I found the thank-you response card from Jackie.

Clara has every newspaper article that she ever appeared in. Whenever Clara didn't agree with something or someone, she wrote a letter or spoke out about it. Clara has all of her postcards that she wrote to her coworkers during her travels. Her travels included over twenty-seven countries, and all around the United States. She must have asked her coworkers to save the postcards for her for when she returned. Clara would make lists, too. All the lists were alphabetized: names, quotes, places, and people, etc. She had cut out cartoons from the newspaper and assigned people's names to them. If she thought that the comic reminded her of someone, she assigned that person's name to the comic.

I find several stories about Clara's family typed by her on a typewriter. It's funny to see typing errors that she tried to correct. I wonder if she was working on a book at one point or if they were papers written for school.

I also find all the information regarding her injury on the city bus and all the letters she wrote complaining about her eye surgery. In addition, she has all the reports from every doctor appointment she had; her health history is completely chronicled. Every story Clara told me is here and documented; it's all so interesting.

I feel sad that she must have been so lonely the past twenty years or so, after having a life that was so active and full of school, work, family, friends, clubs, travels, political events, and volunteering. What happened to the Clara who had enjoyed all of this?

Headstone

Tom from the funeral home calls to give me the phone number for Stan the headstone mason. I need to get Clara's stone made. I call Stan and tell him about the request Clara had made for a stone to match her parents'. Stan tells me that he needs to go to the cemetery to take a look and he'll get back to me. I tell him that Clara is buried next to her sister and to look at her sister's stone, too.

Stan goes to the cemetery and calls me with two options. He can do a stone like her parents' or a stone like her sister's. Both stones are quite large. However, a stone like her parents' will be few hundred dollars more than a stone like her sister's. Her parents' stone is slightly larger, and is made from a different mineral type. I start to agonize. In addition to the stone selection, I have to figure out what to write on it.

I talk to Joy about my anxieties. Joy tries to reassure me that whatever I select will be fine. She also offers to stop by the cemetery and get some pictures of the wording on both Clara's parents' stone and her sister's the following week when she is in Superior. I thank her. Perhaps this will help me know what to have Stan write.

After she returns, Joy emails me the pictures. There is Hebrew writing on her parents' stone. If I go with a stone like her parents', I'll need Clara's Hebrew name. Clara told me and the rabbi this information a few days before she died. However, I can't be sure that I heard her correctly, and I'm not sure if I can read her handwriting on the sheet of paper she wrote it on. I email her nephew, too, to ask his opinion. Like Joy, he says that whatever I select will be fine. I also make a phone call to Valerie. Since she knew Clara, I think that maybe she will have some insights for me. I'm so worried about making a mistake.

It's seems strange that I have to pick out a headstone for Clara. Valerie says I should do what Clara asked. Clara had asked for a stone like her parents', but she is buried next to her sister. I decide on the stone type to match her parents', but on the size to match her sister's. Both Stan and I think the smaller size will look better next to her sister's stone. I ask Stan to send me two proposals: one with the Hebrew, and one without. I receive the proposals in the mail. It is $150.00 more to do the stone with the extra Hebrew writing on it. Great—another thing for me to worry about.

I keep staring at the two sketches that Stan has sent me and ask myself if Clara's stone will look better with the writing in Hebrew or without it. Would anyone obsess over this as much as I do? I continue to agonize until I realize that it's time to get another opinion.

I go over to the synagogue and meet with the rabbi to see if he can read the Hebrew writing on Clara's father's stone and give me some advice. The rabbi points out a spelling error on her father's stone. I wonder if anyone has ever noticed this. Making a mistake on Clara' stone is a fear that I have. As does everyone else, the rabbi asks me why I'm worrying so much about it. Good question; I wonder this myself.

I'm going to think like Clara now. It would cost $150.00 extra for the Hebrew writing on her stone, and since I'm not actually sure of Clara's Hebrew name, I think putting that extra $150.00 into her children's fund is a better idea.

After several weeks of worrying and bugging Stan with questions, I make my selection.

Valerie

I'm meeting with Valerie today and I'm so excited to
show her the many things that I've found of Clara's. We
sit on the floor in Clara's apartment and look through
some of Clara's photos and letters. As with Joy, Valerie
and I also share Clara stories. We laugh and cry together.
I thought I did crazy things for and with Clara, but
Valerie's relationship with her tops mine!

I tell Valerie the story of when I returned to Clara's
apartment after grocery shopping on the day I received a
coupon for free milk at the checkout counter and Clara
said, "Did you get me the milk?" I tell Valerie that I
hadn't, and that Clara asked me to go back to the grocery
store and use her coupon to get her the free gallon of
milk. Valerie tells me that she and Clara did this a lot.
However, Clara would have them go out to the car, and
then she would send Valerie back in for the milk on a
separate transaction. The story makes me wonder why
Clara didn't ask me to do this at the time. I still think she
may have tricked me that day, although I suppose she

could have just found that her milk was indeed sour and then decided she needed more. I'll never know.

Valerie tells me that she and Clara loved each other, and that Clara had said, "I love you" to her. Clara loved someone? I'm shocked, but at the same time happy to hear that Clara was able to express that to someone. I never saw this side of Clara. Last summer during the days following the fire in Clara's building, Valerie wanted Clara to come stay with her. I have often wondered about this. It now makes sense; they cared deeply for one another. Valerie was also able to say no to Clara on many levels. Valerie says that occasionally she'd tell Clara that she would not take her to more than one store at a time. I wish I had been able to say that more often to Clara.

It feels good to talk to another person who had experiences with Clara. Our time spent with Clara was very unique. Valerie tells me that it was very difficult for her to deal with Clara after she moved. Each week, Valerie would make the forty-five-minute drive back to her old building to take Clara shopping and on errands. Clara's expectations were high and it became very tough for Valerie, since she lived so far away.

Valerie says that she has so much regret about all that happened between the two of them. Clara got very mean toward the end, and was especially mean to Valerie. Valerie has tears in her eyes as she tells me this. She was closer to Clara than I understood. I regret not calling Valerie earlier and having her help me go through Clara's things. Maybe it would have helped her feel better about their relationship. From what I know about Clara, Clara was probably angry at Valerie for moving and did not agree with her decision to leave.

Clara had a hard time understanding people's decisions and situations. I think Clara's way of dealing with things was to get annoyed and say hurtful things. I tell Valerie that Clara was very crabby toward the end. She tells me that Clara wasn't always that way. Finding out more about their relationship makes me sad for Valerie. Valerie is a remarkable and special woman; I'm upset with Clara for pushing her away.

Before Valerie leaves, I give her Clara's personalized tools that I found when going through her things. Clara had a wrench, hammer, and pliers with her name on it. I didn't want to sell or donate these. Valerie lived next to Clara and probably fixed many more things around Clara's apartment than I ever did. It is only fitting that the tools should go to Valerie. I also give Valerie back the plants that she had given to Clara. I have taken special care of these plants, knowing that I would return them to Valerie.

Family

I've been asked to fill in for a teacher who is on leave from a local preschool. Managing my time between settling Clara's estate, doing my own accounting work, and subbing at the preschool will clearly be a challenge. However, when it comes to helping out at the preschool, I never turn down the opportunity. Like Clara, I enjoy spending time with children.

I am working with the three-year-olds twice a week, and students at this age don't recognize my dyslexia. I'm a bit quirky in my teaching, and the students seem to enjoy my odd and unorganized ways of running the class. In the older grades, which I have taught in Sunday school, one or two students will always correct my errors when I read a book out loud to the class. I blush when this happens; however, I enjoy seeing the proud looks on their faces when they realize that they can read as well as, if not better than, their teacher.

In one of the classes, there is an adorable set of twin boys who look very familiar to me. I can't figure out how I know them, though. After a few weeks of teaching, I ask their teacher their names. I'm shocked when I realize that they're Clara's cousins. I had seen their pictures when looking through all of Clara's family photos over the summer. Clara would have loved the twins, and in turn I know the boys would have gotten a kick out of her, too. The twins are bright, inquisitive, creative, and funny. I have a clear picture in my mind of the entertaining time Clara would have had with them, the boys proudly showing Clara their artwork, and Clara nodding with approval.

As I watch the students during an indoor playtime, one of the twins walks up to me and asks if I would walk with him over to where the toys are stored. He wants me to help him look for a particular toy. As we walk, he reaches up to hold my hand. Holding hands, we walk together to the toys. I turn my head away so that he doesn't see me cry. I cry for Clara's loss of not knowing her wonderful little cousins. I feel blessed to have met the twins and their family! Through them, I have learned more about Clara.

Clara had a very large extended family that reached out to her over the last several years. It was sad for me to learn that she chose to isolate herself and miss out on many wonderful family opportunities.

Preschool

I have been wanting to talk to Patti about the apple
orchard field trip that Clara spoke about during our first
tax season together back in March 2011. Clara told me
the story while we were waiting for her to meet with
the accountant. As Clara told it, she gave one of the
students an apple and Patti grabbed it away. Clara was
not describing the beloved preschool teacher that I knew.
All of my children attended the preschool, and Patti was
their teacher. I had spent a lot of time in the classroom
and I knew Patti's teaching skills to be next to none! My
kids adored her, and still have wonderful memories of her
and the preschool. I'm so curious about the story, and it's
been bugging me for over a year now.

I contact Patti and ask if she wants to meet for coffee
to talk about Clara. She does, and when we meet, Patti
tells me that Clara volunteered for twelve years in her
classroom and then talks about the field trip to the apple
orchard. The classes were on a tight schedule during
the field trip. The students had just finished sampling
the apples in one of the rooms and were getting ready

to leave. Clara continued to give apples to the students as they were all leaving. Patti asked Clara several times to not give any more apples to the students. But Clara continued on, ignoring Patti's request. Patti knew Clara's personality well and also knew that Clara wanted to make use of all the apples so they did not go to waste. Clara was not happy about leaving the extra apples.

Wow! This sounds like the Clara I knew from our shopping escapades and from her stories about growing up around a grocery store. After the incident, Clara told Patti that she was not coming back to volunteer. Seriously, not returning to volunteer because of an apple? If Clara had not died, would my demise have been over a piece of fruit, too? It was obvious to Patti that Clara did not agree with her during the field trip. This is another one of the same stories that I've heard so often from the people who knew Clara. It's another door closed by Clara for such a ridiculous reason.

Patti also tells me that during the years Clara volunteered in the classroom, Clara would speak her mind. If she thought there was something wrong with a student, Clara would say, "What's wrong with him/her?" I was sad to hear this, but at the same time not surprised. I remember the very first day I met Clara. She mentioned out loud to Allison, the social worker, that I was small and that she was expecting someone older.

I was hoping to hear that Clara had had some sense while being around the students in the classroom. Patti says that she would whisper to Clara and ask her not to talk like that in front of the students. Clara would never listen to Patti's suggestions, which is not surprising to me, either. But Patti also tells me that the students enjoyed Clara's company and looked forward to her reading and playing games with them.

When I went through Clara's things, I found several dozen awards and recognition certificates that she had received from the school district. She spent many years volunteering at the elementary level, too. Clara had well over one hundred thank-you cards, colored pictures, and drawings from the students, thanking her for being in the classroom. From what I read, Clara loved to play checkers and the students enjoyed it as much, if not more. I think the children were too young to recognize Clara's oddities. But if they did, they still loved her nonetheless.

Patti also tells me that Clara would only speak with her and would not speak with any of the other teachers at the preschool. There were two classrooms, and Clara would only help in Patti's room. She never once went into the other room. Patti is describing the Clara that I knew. Clara was very selective about the people she would acknowledge and to whom she would give her time. I find out that Clara was volunteering at the preschool when my children were there. I can only imagine what she was saying about them! Knowing the importance Clara placed on education, it's funny to think that maybe Clara lectured Margie about college back in preschool—well, maybe not about college, but definitely about the importance of education.

Closing

It's a few days before the closing on Clara's condominium and I decide to make a quick stop at her place to make sure everything is okay. I open all the closets and cabinets that I spent so many months cleaning out. In two cabinets I find more junk. *What is this?!* I went through every single one of these cabinets before; where did this extra stuff come from? I sometimes think Clara is still adding to her collection.

Clara's blue jacket—the one that she wore on most of our shopping days—still hangs in her closet. I grab it on my way out, but keep it in my car for a couple of days, trying to decide what to do with it. I don't have it in my heart to throw it away.

I finally decide to make a ceremonial trip over to the Goodwill to donate it.

Once there, I get out of my car and reluctantly hand the jacket to the attendant who is on duty receiving the donations. But letting go of it is harder that I thought it would be; I break down crying in my car as I leave the Goodwill parking lot. I pull over and get out to go back and retrieve the jacket. I stand near my car, trying to clear my head; I know that I have to let the jacket go. I get back in my car and drive away, leaving Clara's blue jacket behind.

Today is the closing on Clara's condominium, and my car won't start. My battery is dead. I wonder if Clara has something to do with this. I need to get to the condominium before the closing to pick up a couple items that I have left there.

I get my battery replaced and rush over to Clara's. I quickly grab all the remaining items in the condominium and place them in the hallway. I check my watch and realize that I have a few extra minutes before I need to leave. I walk through every room and think of Clara. I have spent so much time here both with and without Clara. Soon, all of the money Clara meticulously saved will be in the hands of the right people, the people who will make sure that Clara's beloved children receive the benefit of her thoughtfulness.

I walk to the door, turning only once to look at the chair, sitting alone in the living room. I take a deep breath, and walk out. I close the door behind me, taking with me the memories of a most remarkable woman, a woman who would forever change my life. A woman named Clara.

After

It took almost two years to finalize Clara's estate. The first six months were a whirlwind of financial complexities— on top of a cleaning and deodorizing fest. Settling her estate was extremely time consuming, complicated, and very stressful. Just when I would think it was over, things would appear out of thin air. Each time I would laugh, thinking that Clara was doing this because she was not ready to let go. Had I know it was going to be like that when Clara asked me to be her PR, I'm not sure I would have said yes.

Looking back on all of this, I'm not sure which was more difficult: shopping with Clara or cleaning up after her. At times she was frustrating to be with, but in many ways also wonderful to be with. I am sure many people who knew her experienced Clara this way as well.

It took me over a year before I was able to walk into a grocery store without thinking about Clara. When I would see an elderly women shopping, I would feel panic and anxiety. I could not go to banks without thinking about her. Each time I would go near a hospital or medical clinic, I would feel anxious. I cried a lot that year. Maybe it was Clara's death, or all the work on top of my other responsibilities that settling her estate required of me, but my emotional state was pretty fragile, and the memories make me shudder.

I didn't have it in me to be an outreach volunteer for another client. I was and still am too fearful of getting so involved with someone again in that way. I am instead now a hospice volunteer. Clara taught me many things in life and death. Clara was very sick the last four months of her life. I did not realize it then, but Clara would have qualified for hospice a lot sooner than a couple of days before she died.

I did keep one thing of Clara's for myself: a hardcover book, *The Good Earth* by Pearl S. Buck, published 1931. Clara signed it in 1937. Clara would have been nineteen years old. For some strange reason, when I went to donate all of her books, I grabbed this one from the bag and tossed it in my car. I had—and have—no clear idea why I did that. Something just told me to keep it. I had never read the book and didn't know anything about the story.

The Good Earth sat in the back of my truck for several months. It was stained and had a terrible musty smell, just like all of Clara's things. I eventually took it out of my car and put it in my screened porch. I didn't want it inside my house because of its smell. I would periodically glance through the window at the old book to make sure it was still there. Every once in a while, I would pick it up and check the smell. I wasn't sure what my intent was for the book. The book sat out in the porch for an entire year.

One summer evening, I picked it up it and began to read. I thought of Clara as a young woman, reading the book. I wondered if the book had been required reading for a college course or if she read it for pleasure. Either way, I couldn't help but think that Clara took some great meaning from this book, with its themes of frugality, hard work, and being strong. The book somehow gave me more answers to who Clara was, and reading it was a closure to a very long and difficult year.

Reviewing my journal from all the time that I spent with Clara—and from the time that I spent cleaning up after her—has also helped me move on and let go of the craziness of that period in my life. I now see it all as an important step in my understanding of myself, of the significance of relationships, and of the value of a life lived at least in part for others. While the cost of learning this was great, it is a lesson that I'll never let go of.

Acknowledgments

Jody, your guidance helped me begin the process of turning my journal into the story of Clara and me, and our time spent allowed me to reexamine where I really wanted to go with that story. I thank you for this. Jennifer, I'm blessed that my journey led me to you. You encouraged me to explore new areas, and not be afraid. Most importantly, you understood who I was and what I needed to say. Thank you for it all! Alicia, thank you for reviewing my manuscript and happily embracing my continuous revisions. Your guidance through this process has been invaluable. Abbey, thank you for making me laugh. You brought Clara to life in way that I know she would have approved. Thank you to Laura for being open to my ever-changing ideas, and being able to create something wonderful from this. To Beaver's Pond Press, thank you for your guidance and mentoring. The process has been a wonderful experience. Thank you to Larry for stepping in at such at such a critical time. To Mark, I can't say enough; thank you so much for being there when I needed you the most! Thank you to the Jewish Family and Children's Service of Minneapolis, Sholom Community Alliance, and the Minneapolis Jewish Federation for the support you provided to both Clara and me. Thank you to Ellen, for all your hard work with those crazy transfers! Beverly, my adventures with Clara started in our first meeting. Thank you for supporting and listening to me along the way. Endless gratitude to my good friends Jan, Tammi, and Lea. Patti, I can't thank you enough. You're a very special part of my story. Sue, you're wonderful, thank you for keeping me on track. Betty, thank you for a walk down memory lane! Amy, you cheered me on from the start, were on the sidelines along the way, and carried me to the finish; I'm forever grateful. Thank you to all the banks, grocery stores, pharmacies, etc., that both Clara and I frequented. Thank you to Clara's family for your support and your trust in me to do the right thing for Clara. A heartfelt thank you to Joy and Valerie for everything you ever did for Clara all those years—and a big thanks to you for listening and supporting me through all the chaos and craziness. To my family and friends, thank you for listening to my Clara stories!

Clara left a legacy, and her special act of generosity will never be forgotten.

She was one of a kind, and knowing her was a gift.

Clara, thank you for our story!

BETH, YOUR VOLUNTEER